Whole 30 Slow Cooker Cookbook

Over 110 Top Easy & Delicious Slow Cooker Recipes Made for Your Crock-Pot Cooking At Home Or Anywhere

By Danna Julie

TABLE OF CONTENTS

INTRODUCTION

Let me start your journey by thanking you and expressing my utmost gratitude and appreciation for purchasing this book.

While writing this book, my core aim was to ensure that readers of all stages of Cook were able to grasp the concept of Whole30 diet and Slow Cooker. In doing so, I tried my best to keep this book as simple and easy to understand as possible.

The whole book has been divided into bite-sized sections. Each of those sections focuses on a single topic. The beginning of the book focuses on explaining the ins and outs of Whole30, then the basics of using a slow cooker. And finally, you can explore the Whole30 slow cooker recipes.

I hope you enjoy the book and live your Whole30 diet and slow cooker experience to the fullest. Have a good day and be safe!

CHAPTER 1: BASICS OF WHOLE30

The underlying concept of this amazing program was introduced to the world, back in 2009, by the now world famous medical practitioners Melissa Hartwig and Dallas Hartwig. Since the dieter following this program tends to let go of various food groups, the Whole30 diet is also referred to as "Elimination Diet" by some individuals.

The fundamental objective of this program was to reset the internal metabolic system of your body by putting it through a meticulously-crafted and balanced diet program for 30 days. This carefully planned program will allow your body to re-invigorate itself and improve the metabolic defensive and digestive mechanisms; making them healthier and stronger. You will experience drastic improvements to your physical and psychological health.

The method through which Whole30 diet works is a practical and logical one. During the 30 days of the Whole30 program, you will be letting go of various food groups that have been known to cause harm to your body. Foods such as processed, some dairy products, sugar-dredged foods are among some of the culprits that will be eliminated from your diet. Before long you will be enjoying a clean and healthy diet. This process of elimination allows your body to re-assess the internal mechanism and improve your health in the process.

I know you are probably excited to jump directly into the recipes, but I encourage you to take some time and go through the introductory chapters, as it will allow you to gain a better understanding of the program.

That being said, first things first! Let me first share some of the amazing benefits you are going to experience on Whole30 diet.

ADVANTAGES OF WHOLE30 DIET

Once you embark on a clean diet, and eliminate unhealthy foods from your life, you will enjoy some advantages in the long run. Whole30 diet program provides a healthy transformation that will enhance and improve your life in a positive way. Below are some of the benefits you will have:

- Eliminating sugar from your body, you will experience a more sound and relaxing sleep.
- Experience consistent energy through the day.
- Reduce digestive issues, such as gas, bloating, stomach rumbling.
- Anxiety levels will reduce significantly.
- Condition of your skin will improve.
- Hair will be healthier and shinier.
- Workout sessions will be more effective.
- Will help trim body fat.

WHAT TO EAT

Foods allowed to consume while on Whole30 diet:

- Almond flour
- Almond milk
- Arrowroot Powder
- Bacon
- Bean Sprouts
- Cacao
- Canola Oil
- Olive Oil
- Carob
- Chia
- Citric Acid

- Coconut Flour
- Coconut Water
- Coffee
- Dates
- Flax Seed
- Fruit Juice
- Guar Gum
- Green Beans
- Hemp Seeds
- Lara bars

- Mayonnaise (Homemade)
- Mustard
- Nutritional Yeast
- Potatoes (Added in August 2014)
- Salt
- Sunflower Oil
- Snow Peas
- Tahini
- Water Kefir
- Eggs

Following food groups allowed:

- Vegetables
- Fruits

- Meat
- Seafood

- Nuts and Seeds
- Oils and Ghee

WHAT TO AVOID

These are to be avoided during the 30 days:

- Amino Acids

- Buckwheat

- Carob

- Deep Fried Chips
- Dark Chocolate
- Chewing Gum
- Hummus
- Paleo Bread
- Paleo Ice Cream
- Pancakes
- Any kind of Protein Shakes
- Quinoa
- Stevia Leaf
- Vanilla Extract

Food groups to avoid:

- Dairy products, such as cow's milk, cream, yogurt, kefir, butter, etc. (only clarified butter/ghee is allowed).
- Grains, such as corn, wheat, quinoa, millet.
- Alcoholic Beverages
- Legumes, such as peas, lentils, peanuts, and soy products, such as tofu, miso, Edamame.

SYMPTOMS TO RECOGNIZE

Generally speaking, the Whole30 program does not come with any side effects. However, you should keep in mind your body will be going through a significant change since you will be eliminating a good deal of food groups your body has become used to consuming.

This change will cause you to experience a number of symptoms. These symptoms usually show up within the first 14 days of the diet and soon go away once the body habituates itself to the new diet.

- Minor headaches
- Feeling lethargic
- Sleepiness
- Crankiness
- Brain Fog
- Food Cravings
- Minor Breakouts
- Minor Bloating

With all of those out of the way, here are some tips you should keep in mind in order to make your Whole30 journey as pleasant as possible.

TIPS ON SUCCESSFUL JOURNEY

The following tips will help to ensure you experience a pleasant and smooth Whole30 journey:

- Fully set your mind and commit to the journey.
- Plan the first 2 weeks. Breaking down the journey will make it easier to maintain the experience.
- Clear out the house of any foods are non-Whole30 compliant.
- Plan meals ahead of time.
- Mix and match meals to create your perfect plan.
- Use recipes provided in this book as well.
- Set one day aside to prepare meals in advance.

- Try to keep food-related socializing events at a minimum.
- The Whole30 community is full of inspiring stories. If you start feeling left out, browse the web, you will find a plethora of support materials.
- Try to keep yourself distracted from food cravings.
- And most importantly, never give up.

WHAT TO DO AFTER THE 30 DAYS?

This is perhaps the part of the Whole30 program that confuses most people. Once you are done with the 30 days challenge, what are you supposed to do then?

Well, the first 30 days were actually only the first phase of the program. There are 3 more phases to follow. I will be writing all the phases below to give you a clear idea of what you should do moving forward.

STEP 2: REINTRODUCTION

The second step of the program is known as "Reintroduction." This is a crucial and important phase of the diet.

So here's the thing, once you complete the first phase of the diet, you are now tasked to make a meal plan for the upcoming 10 days where you will be re-introducing some of the food groups you have been avoiding for the past 30 days.

Throughout this gradual introduction of the food groups, you will get the opportunity to assess how each food group affects your metabolic levels and evaluate which foods are healthy for your diet.

The plan of re-introduction usually require you to re-introduce 1 food group at a time, to ensure you are still heavily relying on your Whole30 diet.

The re-introduction phase is often seen as a scientific trial that helps you asses which food groups are better for your body and which are not.

You should keep in mind though that it is not recommended to experiment with multiple food groups at the same time. As an example, you can only experiment with peanut butter or jam, not both.

During this phase, you should pay close attention to how the body reacts to the food groups.

A sample meal plan might look the one below:

Day 1: Start off by re-introducing legumes and evaluate how your body metabolizes them.

Day 4: After a 3-day trial, select the legumes you want to keep. Move on to non-gluten grains; corn tortilla chips or white rice.

Day 7: This should be followed by an evaluation of dairy products; cheese or ice cream.

Day 10: Finally, you should evaluate gluten –containing grains to see how your body reacts.

You should also stick to your Whole30 diet while experimenting with food.

STEP 3: SHARE YOUR EXPERIENCE

Ever since the conception of Whole30 program, the program has created a massive following which has led to a very helpful and ever-growing community.

So, once you have completed your Whole30 challenge, it is recommended you share your experience with the community.

You have no idea how much of an impact your story might make on someone else's life.

Here are some pointers to put your journey into words:

- How you gained control over your food eating habits.
- How Whole30 helped eliminate various symptoms or conditions.
- How biomarkers such as triglycerides, blood pressure, or blood sugar levels improved.
- How Whole30 diet helped trim down your weight and gain confidence.
- How it helped you to become pregnant.
- How Whole30 helped you to be at peace with yourself.
- How you were able to transfer Whole30 habits to other aspects of your life.

STEP 4: UPCOMING JOURNEY

One thing to keep in mind is that you should never think the 30 days of your Whole30 challenge as being the end of the diet. Rather, you should look at it as being a new beginning to a healthier lifestyle.

While you won't be able to completely eradicate the damage done to your body in the past, but you can definitely get onto healthy path for the future.

The following strategies should help you to keep following the Whole30 journey well beyond your 30 days.

- Focus on Whole30-based meals every single day as long as you can without breaks or "cheat day." Should the hunger for sugar come creeping back in, choose something very small, enough for the craving to pass. But don't deter from your path.

- Should you stumble across something irresistible, or something culturally or religiously important to you, make a small exception. You also want to assess if the food is actually worth it. If it helps, then you can follow the guide below that will help you assess the food and decide if eating it would be a good idea.

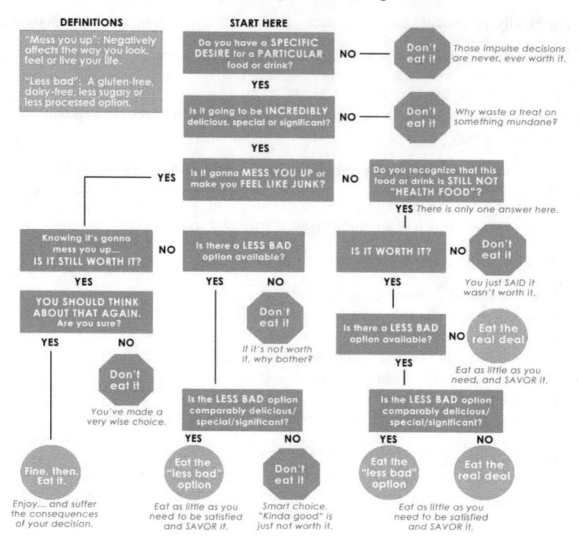

- Assuming you have decided to have the treat, make sure to take your time while eating the meal. Eat consciously; trying to maintain your diet as much possible. A good way to do this is to eat just a little. Discard any uneaten portion to remove temptation later.
- Don't feel guilt or shame for the craving. What is done is done. Keep yourself together and move forward; stick to your Whole30 program.

Since the recipes provided in this book are Whole30 slow cooker recipes, the next chapter will focus on the fundamentals of the slow cooker appliance itself.

CHAPTER 2: UNDERSTANDING YOUR SLOW COOKER

If you are already an expert in the art of slow Cook, then you can skip this chapter and begin exploring the recipes. However, if you are planning on embarking into the world of slow cooker for the first time, then you will find this chapter useful. That being said, let's start with the basics.

WHAT IS A SLOW COOKER?

Let me clear up one major confusion. Slow cookers and crockpots are usually the same appliance. If you see a book with "crockpot," and another book with "slow cooker" in the title, both of them are usually referring to the same thing. The main difference is that the Crock-Pot is now the most popular brand of slow cooker. So not all slow cookers are Crock-Pots, but all Crock-Pots are Slow Cookers.

The core functionality of a slow cooker is to produce mouthwatering and enticing meals by cooking them over low temperature for an extended period of time. Despite common belief, slow cookers are versatile in nature and you can create almost anything using the slow cooker, ranging from roasts, dips, stews, desserts.

Looking at the basic components of the slow cooker, you will notice it consists of an oval-shaped Cook pot mostly made out of high quality glazed ceramic or porcelain. This is the housing where all the internal circuitry is being held.

A glass lid is also provided with the cooker to allow the appliance to be closed properly by sitting in the grooves around the edge of the pot. The condensed vapor produced inside the pot allows the device to create a low yet effective pressure seal that helps the lid stay in place.

However, it should be noted that slow cookers are safer to use when compared to other counter appliances, such as pressure cookers. As slow cookers cook on low pressure.

ADVANTAGES TO USING A SLOW COOKER

When comparing slow cooker with other traditional methods of Cooking appliance, there are certain advantages to enjoy. Some of the notable ones are as follows:

- Slow cookers indirectly help you to control the temptation of ordering take out. Since you will be able to cook a wide variety of meals with absolute ease.
- Slow cookers allow you to prepare meals throughout the year. A slow cooker provides you the opportunity to enjoy summer and winter meals all the time.
- Slow cookers utilize a process that cooks meals at a slow temperature and over an extended period of time, which tenderizes less-expensive cuts of meat, adding flavor.
- Slow Cook meals extracts the full array of flavors and allows you to try a wide variety of meals such as soups, stews, casseroles. The possibilities are numerous.

There are also certain things new users should be aware of. To ensure you don't go through the same mistakes as others, the section below will help you to stay on the right path and enhance your slow Cook life.

MISTAKES TO AVOID USING A SLOW COOKER

- Avoid opening the lid while Cook.
- Avoid adding dairy too early.
- Avoid exceeding recommended level of liquid.

BUYING YOUR FIRST SLOW COOKER

Chances are good you have already purchased a slow cooker, or planning to buy one. This brief section will provide a brief guide to choose the right slow cooker for you and your family. The following factors to consider:

Heat Distribution: choose one that has a good heat distribution choices.

The Lid: Transparent lid; easy to check progress of food Cook and avoid lifting the lid.

Size: Yes it is important. Choose your cooker according to requirement of your family.

Hob-Safe: If you are planning on Cook meat frequently, choose a cooker made of ceramic.

THE TOP COOKERS AT THE MOMENT:

Lakeland 1.5 liter Slow Cooker — 28$ —Perfect for small families and couples.

Morphy Richards Sear and Stew Compact — 66$ — Space efficient, simple to use.

Russell Hobbs 3.5l Slow Cooker — 32$ — Perfect for family, offers best value for money.

Crock Pot 5.6l Slow and Multi Cooker — 161$ — Premium model. Crock pot company made the first slow cooker on the market and their contemporary models are amazing.

SLOW COOK TIMES

- If a meal normally takes 15-30 minutes, then it would take 1-2 hours on high setting or 4-6 hours on low setting in your crock pot.
- If a meal normally takes 30-60 minutes, then it would take 2-3 hours on high setting or 5-7 hours on low setting in your crock pot.
- If a meal normally takes 1-2 hours, then it would take 4-6 hours on high setting or 6-8 hours on low setting in your crock pot.
- If a meal normally takes 2-4 hours, then it would take 4-6 hours on high setting or 8-12 hours on low setting in your crock pot.

That being said, you are now ready to venture into the amazing world of Slow Cook!

SLOW COOK SAVES TIME

Slow cookers come equipped with a sophisticated timer mechanism. The cookers eliminate the need of you to stand in front of the cooker the whole day until the food is cooked. With these appliances, you can add the ingredients and chill out until the meal is ready. Once the meal is ready, the slow cooker will turn itself off to avoid overcook. This will save a lot of time during your day, and allow you to use that time to enjoy life or develop yourself for a better tomorrow? The options are limitless.

Now, on to the recipes. These should give you a good base to get started on your Whole30 slow cooker journey. Hope you enjoy them.

Chapter 3: Beef Recipes

Beef And Mushroom Gravy

(Prep time: 13 minutes\ Cook time: 8 hours\ 8 Servings)

Ingredients

- 2 medium onions, peeled, sliced
- 2 pounds boneless beef round steak, slice in 8 portions
- 3 cups sliced mushrooms
- 1 cup sliced turnips
- 1 jar beef gravy
- 1 envelope dry mushroom gravy mix

Directions

1. Lay onions along bottom of slow cooker, place slices of steak on top
2. Top with sliced turnips
3. Combine beef gravy, mushroom gravy in a bowl, stir
4. Pour in slow cooker
5. Cover with lid, and cook on SLOW 8 hours
6. Serve with mashed potatoes

Nutrition Values (Per Serving)

- Calories: 1336
- Fat: 85g
- Carbohydrates: 21g
- Protein: 112g

Short Ribs

(Prep time: 10 minutes\ Cook time: 6 hours\ 3 Servings)

Ingredients:

- 1 beef short rib
- 2 small red onion
- 2 minced garlic cloves
- 1 teaspoon ground ginger
- 2 pieces star anise
- 1 tablespoon date paste

Preparation:

1. Chop the onion and crush the garlic
2. Add the beef to your slow cooker
3. Add garlic, onion, ginger, date paste and star anise on top
4. Add 1 cup water to slow cooker
5. Cover with lid, and cook on SLOW 6 hours
6. Once done, season and serve with your veggies!

Nutrition Values (Per serving)

- Calories: 105
- Fat: 7g
- Carbohydrates: 0g
- Protein: 11g

Sweet And Spicy Potato Chili

(Prep time: 15 minutes\ Cook time: 4 hours\ 6 Servings)

Ingredients:

- 2 pounds ground beef
- 1 minced garlic clove
- 1 diced onion
- 2 cans tomato sauce
- 1 can minced tomatoes

- 3 cups beef broth
- 2 large peeled, diced sweet potatoes
- 3-4 tablespoon chili powder
- 2 teaspoon black pepper
- ¼ teaspoon oregano
- Cilantro for garnish

Directions

1. Heat a large skillet, brown the ground beef. Drain any excess fat
2. Transfer cooked beef to slow cooker, and add rest of listed Ingredients
3. Stir well
4. Cover with lid, and cook on SLOW 4 hours
5. Serve on a platter, garnish with cilantro

Nutrition Values (Per Serving)

- Calories: 210
- Fat: 8g
- Carbohydrates: 20g
- Protein: 15g

BEEF TONGUE TACOS

(Prep time: 10 minutes\ Cook time: 8 hours\ 4 Servings)

Ingredients:

- 1 yellow onion, cut into large slices
- 1 x 5 pound beef tongue
- 1 teaspoon sea salt
- 1 teaspoon black pepper
- ½ teaspoon garlic powder
- ½ teaspoon chipotle chili powder
- ¼ teaspoon white pepper
- Large lettuce leaves for wraps

Topping

- 1 jar pico de gallo
- 1-2 cups guacamole

Directions

1. Place onion slices along bottom of slow cooker
2. Sprinkle and rub seasoning over beef tongue
3. Transfer to cooker
4. Add enough water to cover meat
5. Cover with lid, and cook on LOW 8 hours
6. Once meat is cooked, remove, pull off skin
7. Discard skin and onions
8. Shred the meat, and place in lettuce wraps
9. Top with pico de gallo and guacamole

Nutrition Values (Per Serving)

- Calories: 195
- Fat: 4g
- Carbohydrates: 16g
- Protein: 15g

BREAKFAST CASSEROLE

(Prep time: 10 minutes\ Cook time: 4 hours\ 4 Servings)

Ingredients:

- 1 pound cooked, bacon, chopped
- 1 diced red onion
- 1 diced bell pepper
- 1 tablespoon coconut oil
- 2 medium sweet potatoes, grated
- 2 minced garlic cloves

- 12 eggs
- 1 cup coconut milk
- 1 teaspoon dill
- Pinch crushed red pepper
- Salt, pepper to taste
- Garnish: avocado slices

Directions

1. Grease slow cooker with ghee or coconut oil
2. Combine grated sweet potato and crushed red peppers in a bowl
3. Take a skillet, heat up ghee
4. Sauté garlic, pepper, and onions 3 minutes
5. Spread layer of grated sweet potatoes, onion mixture, bacon crumble
6. Repeat until ingredients used
7. In a bowl, whisk coconut milk, eggs, and seasoning
8. Pour mixture over layers in slow cooker
9. Cover with lid, and cook on LOW 4 hours
10. Cut in rectangles, serve hot with avocado

Nutrition Values (Per Serving)

- Calories: 369
- Fat: 23g
- Carbohydrates: 17g
- Protein: 20g

BIRRIA DE RES

(Prep time: 35 minutes\ Cook time: 8 hours\ 6 Servings)

Ingredients:

- 2 pounds extra lean top round beef roast
- 3 dried guajillo peppers
- 2 dried pasilla chilies
- 2 dried ancho chilies
- 1 teaspoon cumin
- ¼ teaspoon pepper
- 3 minced garlic cloves
- ½ teaspoon salt
- 1½ cups chicken broth
- 4 chopped tomatoes

Directions

1. Take a heavy saucepan and place it over medium heat
2. Add dried chilies and stir fry 3-4 minutes until fragrant
3. Add chicken broth to saucepan
4. Cover, turn off the heat, let it sit 30 minutes
5. Seed and devein the chilies
6. Add chilies, tomatoes, water, garlic, cumin, salt, pepper to a blender, blend until smooth
7. Place roast in slow cooker, pour sauce over meat
8. Cover with lid, cook on LOW 8 hours
9. Shred with forks once cooked

Nutrition Values (Per Serving)

- Calories: 198
- Fat: 12g
- Carbohydrates: 9g
- Protein: 28g

VEGETABLE BEEF

(Prep time: 20 minutes\ Cook time: 8 hours\ 6 Servings)

Ingredients:

- 3-4 pounds beef roast
- ½ teaspoon salt
- ¼ teaspoon pepper
- Flavorless cooking oil
- 1½ pounds red potatoes
- 1 small white onion
- 1½ pounds carrots, peeled, cut
- 1 minced garlic clove
- 1 teaspoon dried thyme
- 1 teaspoon dried oregano
- ⅓ cup balsamic vinegar

Directions

1. Sprinkle seasoning, salt, pepper over the roast
2. Place a pan over medium high heat, heat the oil
3. Brown roast on all sides
4. Transfer roast to slow cooker
5. Add diced onion and potatoes around roast
6. Drizzle balsamic and vinegar over roast, add the carrots on top
7. Cover with lid, and cook on LOW 8 hours
8. Once cooked, shred the meat, and serve with potatoes, carrots, onions
9. Drizzle cook juice over top

Nutrition Values (Per Serving)

- Calories: 300
- Fat: 8g
- Carbohydrates: 26g
- Protein: 24g

MEATBALLS

(Prep time: 15 minutes\ Cook time: 4 hours\ 6 Servings)

Ingredients:

Meatballs

- 1¼ pound lean ground beef (85% lean)
- 1 egg
- ¼ cup blanched almond flour
- ¾ teaspoon sea salt
- 2 teaspoon onion powder
- ½ teaspoon garlic powder
- 1 tablespoon Italian seasoning blend
- Pinch crushed red pepper
- 1 tablespoon chopped fresh parsley

Marinara

- 1 can (28 oz) crushed tomatoes with basil
- 1 can (14 oz) diced tomatoes with basil and garlic
- 1 can (6 ounce) tomato paste
- 2 cloves fresh garlic, chopped
- 2 tablespoons chopped fresh oregano leaves
- 2 bay leaves
- Pinch of sea salt, pepper

Directions

1. Take a small bowl and add almond flour, onion, ½ a teaspoon salt, onion, Italian seasoning, red pepper, garlic powder, mix well

2. Take a large bowl and add ground beef
3. Add the egg and almond mixture to the beef, and mix well
4. Using your hand, form 20 meatballs from mixture
5. Take a large baking sheet and line with parchment paper, pre-heat broiler on oven
6. Broil meatballs 2-4 minutes per side
7. Add the sauce ingredients to slow cooker
8. Add broiled meatballs to cooker, stir
9. Cover with lid, and cook over LOW 4 hours
10. Serve with garnish of fresh herbs

Nutrition Values (Per Serving)

- Calories: 354
- Fat: 17g
- Carbohydrates: 16g
- Protein: 22g

BEEF CHILI

(Prep time: 25 minutes\ Cook time: 6 hours\ 8 Servings)

Ingredients:

- 1 tablespoon avocado oil
- 1 pound grass fed beef
- 1 diced green bell pepper
- 1 diced red bell pepper
- 1 large diced onion
- 2 garlic cloves, chopped
- 1 small sweet potato, peeled, diced
- 1 can (28 oz) crushed tomatoes
- 1 can (14 oz) diced tomatoes (fire roasted)

- 3 tablespoons chili powder
- 1 tablespoon smoked paprika, 1 tablespoon ground cumin
- 2 teaspoon salt
- ½ teaspoon ground cinnamon,½ teaspoon ground chipotle chili
- Garnish: sliced avocado, fresh cilantro

Directions

1. Take a large skillet, heat on medium
2. Heat up oil, add beef and cook 4-6 minutes, break apart as cooking
3. Transfer beef to slow cooker, stir in onion, pepper, potatoes, diced tomatoes, chili powder, smoked paprika, salt, cumin, chipotle, cinnamon
4. Cover with the lid, and cook on HIGH 6 hours
5. Serve with avocado or cilantro

Nutrition Values (Per Serving)

- Calories: 173
- Fat: 5g
- Carbohydrates: 15g
- Protein: 5g

CHUCK ROAST

(Prep time: 20 minutes\ Cook time: 8 hours\ 4 Servings)

Ingredients:

- ⅓ cup olive oil
- 3-4 pounds chuck roast
- 6 carrots, diced
- 3 celery stalks, diced

- 1 large onion, diced
- 4 garlic cloves, minced
- 2 peeled, cubed rutabagas
- 1 cup dried mushrooms
- 1 cup beef broth
- ½ cup fresh basil, ½ cup fresh parsley
- ¼ cup fresh rosemary
- 2 tablespoons balsamic vinegar
- Zest from 1 lemon
- ⅓ cup pine nuts
- Pinch kosher salt, black pepper

Directions

1. Soak dried mushrooms in 1 cup lukewarm water 30 minutes
2. Strain the mushrooms, retain the liquid
3. Pour liquid through a cheesecloth, set aside
4. Heat a large skillet, add pine nuts, stir fry them 10 minutes
5. Transfer pine nuts, fresh herbs, lemon zest, garlic to food processor, pulse well
6. Drizzle in olive oil, pulse until a paste forms
7. Season the roast generously with paste, and salt and pepper
8. In same skillet, heat olive oil over high, sear roast on all sides, transfer to slow cooker
9. Pour broth into the skillet, deglaze skillet, pour liquid over roast
10. Add mushroom liquid, mushrooms, balsamic vinegar, leftover pine nut to cooker
11. Scatter carrots, onion, celery, rutabaga around the roast
12. Cover with lid, and cook on SLOW 8 hours
13. Remove roast and veggies, drizzle cooking juice over ingredients

Nutrition Values (Per Serving)

- Calories: 270
- Fat: 21g
- Carbohydrates: 5g
- Protein: 11g

BEEF STEAK WITH PEPPERS

(Prep time: 10 minutes\ Cook time: 8 hours\ 4 Servings)

Ingredients:

- 8 pieces cubed steak
- 1¾ teaspoon garlic salt
- Pinch of black pepper
- 1 can (8 oz) tomato sauce
- 1 cup water
- 1 red bell pepper, sliced ¼ inch strips
- 1 medium onion, sliced ¼ inch strips
- ⅓ cup green pitted olives + 2 tablespoons brine

Directions

1. Season the beef with garlic salt, pepper
2. Transfer to slow cooker, add onion, red pepper, tomato sauce, olives
3. Pour in 2 cups water
4. Cover with lid, cook on LOW 8 hours
5. Serve over rice

Nutrition Values (Per Serving)

- Calories: 240
- Fat: 12g
- Carbohydrates: 24g
- Protein: 10g

TACO SOUP

(Prep time: 20 minutes\ Cook time: 8 hours\ 6 Servings)

Ingredients:

- 1½ tablespoons ghee
- 1 large onion, diced
- 2 garlic cloves, diced
- 4 bell peppers, diced
- 2 pounds lean ground beef
- 2 tablespoons chili powder, 2 tablespoons cumin
- 2 teaspoons sea salt, black pepper
- 1 teaspoon paprika, 1 teaspoon cinnamon
- ½ teaspoon garlic powder, ½ teaspoon onion powder, ¼ teaspoon cayenne pepper
- 1 can (28 oz) diced tomatoes
- 4 cups vegetable broth
- ¼ cup coconut milk
- 1 cup diced green chilies
- Garnish: sliced jalapeno, diced green onions, avocado, cilantro, lime slices

Directions

1. Take a large sized pan, heat over medium
2. Melt the ghee, sauté onion, garlic, bell peppers 5 minutes
3. Add ground beef to pan, cook until no longer pink

4. Drain the beef, transfer mixture to slow cooker, season with spices, stir
5. Add diced tomatoes, coconut milk, broth, green chilies, stir well
6. Cover with lid, and cook on LOW 8 hours
7. Serve, garnish with toppings

Nutrition Values (Per Serving)

- Calories: 197
- Fat: 5g
- Carbohydrates: 20g
- Protein: 18g

BEEF ROAST WITH RUTABAGA

(Prep time: 20 minutes\ Cook time: 6 hours\ 4 Servings)

Ingredients:

- 1 pound rutabaga, peeled, cubed
- 1 boneless, bottom round beef roast
- ½ teaspoon of salt
- ½ teaspoon black pepper
- 1 sweet onion, sliced
- 2 fennel bulbs, sliced
- 1 cup beef broth

Directions

1. Season roast with salt, pepper
2. Heat a large skillet, sear roast on all sides
3. Transfer roast to slow cooker, add onion, fennel and rutabaga
4. Pour in beef broth
5. Cover with lid, and cook on LOW 6 hours
6. Serve on platter

Nutrition Values (Per Serving)

- Calories: 450
- Fat: 7g
- Carbohydrates: 21g
- Protein: 51g

MONGOLIAN BEEF

(Prep time: 20 minutes\ Cook time: 4 hours, 20 minutes\ 6 Servings)

Ingredients:

- 1 beef roast, 5 pounds
- 3 garlic cloves, grated
- 1 inch fresh ginger, grated
- 1 medium onion, sliced
- ½ cup water
- ½ cup coconut aminos
- 2 tablespoons black pepper
- 1 tablespoon five spice powder
- 1 tablespoon arrowroot powder
- 1 teaspoon red pepper flakes
- 1 teaspoon sesame oil

Directions

1. Add listed ingredients to slow cooker
2. Cover with lid, and cook on LOW 4 hours
3. Remove roast, slice thinly, return to cooker, cook 20 minutes on HIGH
4. Serve on a platter

Nutrition Values (Per Serving)

- Calories: 490
- Fat: 27g
- Carbohydrates: 10g
- Protein: 49g

CHAPTER 4: PORK RECIPES

PORK ROAST
(Prep time: 10 minutes\ Cook time: 8 hours\ 4 Servings)

Ingredients

- 1 large red onion, sliced
- 2 minced garlic cloves
- 2 pounds boneless pork loin roast
- 1 cup water
- 2 tablespoons red wine vinegar
- 2 tablespoons Worcestershire sauce
- ¼ cup tomato juice
- ½ teaspoon salt
- ½ teaspoon black pepper

Directions

1. Arrange onion slices and minced garlic along bottom of slow cooker
2. Place roast on top
3. In a mixing bowl, add rest of ingredients, pour mixture over the roast
4. Cover with lid, and cook on LOW 8 hours
5. Serve with mashed potatoes

Nutrition Values (Per Serving)

- Calories: 361
- Fat: 31g
- Carbohydrates: 43g
- Protein: 31g

PORK ROAST AND SWEET POTATOES
(Prep time: 5 minutes\ Cook time: 6 hours\ 6 Servings)

Ingredients

- 3 pounds pork butt roast
- 2 cups canned cranberries
- 1 medium onion, peeled, diced
- ½ cup orange juice
- 2 tablespoons apple cider vinegar
- ½ teaspoon five spice powder
- Pinch of sea salt
- ½ teaspoon black pepper
- 3 large sweet potatoes, peeled, quartered

Directions

1. Place pork in slow cooker
2. In a bowl, combine onion, cranberries, orange juice, apple cider vinegar, salt, black pepper, five spice powder, mix well
3. Pour mixture over roast, add the potatoes
4. Cover with lid, and cook on LOW 6 hours
5. Serve on platter with a whole30 side

Nutrition Values (Per Serving)

- Calories: 834
- Fat: 56g
- Carbohydrates: 16g
- Protein: 62g

RANCH CARNITAS

(Prep time: 20 minutes\ Cook time: 4 hours\ 4 Servings)

Ingredients:

- 2 pounds bone-in pork shoulder
- 3 tablespoons ranch seasoning
- 1 teaspoon cumin
- ½ teaspoon sea salt
- ¼ teaspoon pepper
- 3 tablespoons ghee
- ½ cup water
- Corn tortillas

Guacamole

- 2 avocados, diced
- 1 tablespoon ranch dressing
- Juice from ½ a lime
- Pinch of salt

Preparation:

1. Rub seasoning all over pork shoulder
2. Transfer to cooker, add the ghee and water
3. Cover with lid, and cook on LOW 4 hours
4. Prepare guacamole as roast cooks, place in fridge
5. Once roast cooked, shred with forks, serve in corn tortillas, top with guacamole

Nutrition Values (Per Serving)

- Calories: 190
- Fat: 11g
- Carbohydrates: 0g
- Protein: 23g

COCONUT PORK

(Prep time: 10 minutes\ Cook time: 4 hours\ 4 Servings)

Ingredients:

- 2 tablespoons coconut oil
- 4 pounds boneless pork shoulder, cut in chunks
- 1 large onion, chopped
- 3 garlic cloves, minced
- 2 tablespoons fresh ginger, grated
- 1 tablespoon mild curry powder
- 1 tablespoon ground cumin
- ½ teaspoon ground turmeric
- 1 can (14 oz) can diced tomatoes
- 1 cup unsweetened coconut milk
- 2 cups chicken broth
- Pinch of salt, pepper
- Garnish: fresh cilantro, diced green onions

Directions

1. In a large skillet, heat coconut oil
2. Season with salt, pepper, sear pork chunks on all sides
3. Transfer chunks to slow cooker
4. Add onion, ginger, garlic, cumin, turmeric, curry to the skillet, sauté 5 minutes. Transfer to slow cooker
5. Cover with lid, and cook on LOW 4 hours

6. Serve on a platter, garnish with cilantro, green onions

Nutrition Values (Per Serving)

- Calories: 231
- Fat: 17g
- Carbohydrates: 4.6g
- Protein: 14g

ROSEMARY PORK CHOPS

(Prep time: 10 minutes\ Cook time: 4 hours\ 4 Servings)

Ingredients:

- 4 butterfly pork chops, boneless
- 1 cup bone broth
- 6 sprigs fresh rosemary
- 1 cup fresh basil leaves
- 1 tablespoon chopped chives
- ½ teaspoon sea salt
- ¼ teaspoon black pepper
- 3 organic Pink Lady apples, chopped
- 1 cup water

Directions

1. Add listed ingredients to slow cooker
2. Cover with lid, cook on LOW 4 hours
3. Serve on a platter

Nutrition Values (Per Serving)

- Calories: 248
- Fat: 8g
- Carbohydrates: 0.7g
- Protein: 39g

HAM AND PARSNIP CHOWDER

(Prep time: 10 minutes\ Cook time: 3 hours\ 4 Servings)

Ingredients:

- 4 parsnips, tops cut off
- 1 large sweet potato, diced
- 1 cup chopped onion
- 1 tablespoon olive oil
- 4 garlic cloves, minced
- 4 basil leaves, stems removed
- ½ teaspoon black pepper
- 3 cups chicken broth
- 1 cup smoked ham, diced
- 1 cup almond milk
- 2 tablespoons potato starch
- 2 tablespoons coconut aminos
- Pinch of salt, pepper
- Garnish: black pepper, fresh herbs, cream

Directions

1. Add parsnip, basil, garlic, olive oil, broth, salt, pepper
2. Cover with lid, and cook on HIGH 2 hours
3. Remove lid, add almond milk, stir in potato starch, coconut aminos, blend with immersion blender
4. Add ham, diced potatoes, stir well
5. Re-cover with lid, and cook on LOW 1 more hour
6. Ladle soup into bowls, garnish with black pepper, herbs, and cream

Nutrition Values (Per Serving)

- Calories: 1315
- Fat: 76g
- Carbohydrates: 62g
- Protein: 92g

PORK RIBS
(Prep time: 5 minutes\ Cook time: 5 hours, 5 minutes\ 5 Servings)

Ingredients:

- 4 pounds baby back pork ribs
- 2 teaspoons Chinese five-spice powder
- ¾ teaspoon garlic powder
- 1 fresh jalapeno, sliced in rings
- 2 tablespoons rice vinegar
- 2 tablespoons coconut aminos
- 1 tablespoon tomato paste

Directions

1. Dice ribs into cooker sized portions
2. In a small bowl, mix Chinese five-spice, garlic powder, salt, pepper together
3. Massage mixture into ribs
4. Add jalapeno rings to the bottom of cooker
5. Add rice vinegar, tomato paste, coconut aminos, stir well
6. Add ribs
7. Cover with lid, and cook on LOW 5 hours
8. Once done, remove ribs, and pour liquid into a heat proof container
9. Let the liquid chill until fat separates
10. Skim off the fat with a spoon, transfer liquid to a pot, bring to a boil
11. Simmer 5 minutes
12. Use liquid as dipping sauce, serve with meat

Nutrition Values (Per Serving)

- Calories: 620
- Fat: 9g
- Carbohydrates: 46g
- Protein: 34g

Spicy Pork

(Prep time: 10 minutes\ Cook time: 6 hours\ 4 Servings)

Ingredients:

- 2 pounds lean pork tenderloin
- 1 onion, diced
- 4 garlic cloves, minced
- 1 cup chicken broth
- 1 tablespoon apple vinegar
- 1 tablespoon paprika
- 1 teaspoon Ancho chili powder
- 1 teaspoon ground cumin
- 1 teaspoon oregano
- ¼ teaspoon cinnamon
- ¼ teaspoon coriander
- Pinch of salt, pepper

Directions

1. In a small bowl, combine the spices
2. Rub mixture over the pork
3. Transfer pork to slow cooker, and cover with onions
4. Add chicken broth, apple vinegar
5. Cover with lid, and cook on LOW 6 hours
6. Shred the meat using 2 forks, serve with cooking juices
7. If you want a crispier pork, broil 2-3 minutes in oven

Nutrition Values (Per Serving)

- Calories: 273
- Fat: 23g
- Carbohydrates: 1.1g
- Protein: 14g

MINIATURE FRANKS

(Prep time: 7 minutes\ Cook time: 3 hours\ 8 Servings)

Ingredients:

- ¼ cup tomato sauce
- 2 tablespoons apple juice
- ⅔ cup apricot preserve
- 2 tablespoons apple cider vinegar
- 3 garlic cloves, minced
- 1 shallot, chopped
- ½ cup chicken broth
- 2 tablespoons coconut aminos
- ¼ teaspoon cayenne pepper
- ¼ teaspoon black pepper
- 2 pounds mini all-beef frankfurters

Directions

1. Add listed ingredients to slow cooker, except the franks
2. Stir, add the franks
3. Cover with the lid, and cook on LOW 3 hours
4. Serve with mustard

Nutrition Values (Per Serving)

- Calories: 307
- Fat: 21g
- Carbohydrates: 20g
- Protein: 10g

PORK ROAST

(Prep time: 10 minutes\ Cook time: 8 hours\ 6 Servings)

Ingredients:

- Pork roast of pork, 3 pounds
- 1 cup bone or vegetable broth
- 6 sprigs fresh rosemary
- 4 sprigs fresh basil
- 1 tablespoon chives, chopped
- ½ teaspoon sea salt
- ¼ teaspoon black pepper
- Three apples; Pink Lady

Directions

1. Add list of ingredients to slow cooker
2. Cover with lid, and cook on LOW 8 hours
3. Remove roast, allow to rest 10 minutes then slice
4. Serve on a platter

Nutrition Values (Per Serving)

- Calories: 248
- Fat: 8g
- Carbohydrates: 0.7g
- Protein: 39g

PINEAPPLE HAM

(Prep time: 8 minutes\ Cook time: 6 hours\ 6 Servings)

Ingredients:

- 2 pound ham steak, diced in bite-size pieces
- 1 pound canned pineapple tidbits
- 2 tablespoons pineapple juice, from can
- 1 cup leeks, chopped
- 2 garlic cloves, minced
- 3 large potatoes, diced
- ½ cup orange marmalade
- ¼ teaspoon paprika
- ¼ teaspoon ground black pepper
- ½ teaspoon dried basil

Directions

1. Place all ingredients in slow cooker
2. Cover with lid, and cook on LOW 6 hours
3. Serve on platter

Nutrition Values (Per Serving)

- Calories: 337
- Fat: 11g
- Carbohydrates: 46g
- Protein: 14g

CHAPTER 5: GOAT AND LAMB RECIPES

LAMB ROAST WITH VEGETABLES

(Prep time: 20 minutes\ Cook time: 6 hours\ 4 Servings)

Ingredients:

- 4 pound, boneless lamb roast
- 1 tablespoon ghee
- ½ cup chicken broth
- 6 garlic cloves, minced
- 2-3 sprigs rosemary, chopped
- 2-3 sprigs thyme
- ¼ cup stone ground mustard
- 2 carrots, peeled, chopped
- 2 parsnips, peeled, chopped
- 2 Yukon gold potatoes, peeled, chopped
- 1 rutabaga, peeled, chopped
- Pinch of salt, pepper

Directions

1. In a large skillet, heat over medium
2. Melt the ghee, season lamb with salt and pepper, sear lamb on all sides in skillet
3. Transfer roast to slow cooker
4. Pour broth in skillet, deglaze bottom, pour over lamb roast
5. In a small bowl, add garlic, rosemary, thyme, mustard. Stir well
6. Transfer the mixture to your slow cooker and use your hand to coat the lamb well
7. Add chopped up veggies to the cooker and arrange them all around
8. Cover with lid, and cook on LOW for 6 hours
9. Remove from cooker, allow to rest 10 minutes before slicing

Nutrition Values (Per Serving)

- Calories: 610
- Fat: 23g
- Carbohydrates: 69g
- Protein: 31g

LAMB SHANKS

(Prep time: 10 minutes\ Cook time: 4 hours\ 3 Servings)

Ingredients:

- 3 medium lamb shanks
- 4 cups of beef broth
- ¼ cup chopped onion
- 3 crushed garlic cloves
- 2 teaspoon ground ginger
- 1 teaspoon red chili flakes
- ¼ cup coconut oil
- 2½ tablespoons chopped basil
- 1 tablespoon oregano leaves
- 2 teaspoons thyme leaves
- Zest from 1 lemon

Directions

1. Take a large skillet, heat over medium
2. Melt coconut oil and fry the lamb shanks
3. Transfer to a bowl
4. Add garlic, onion, ginger along with spices to skillet, cook to soften
5. Add lamb shanks, cooked spices, rest of ingredients to slow cooker
6. Add broth
7. Cover with lid, and cook on HIGH 4 hours, check after 3 hours for doneness
8. Serve on a platter with a Whole30 side

Nutrition Values (Per Serving)

- Calories: 465
- Fat: 24g
- Carbohydrates: 8g
- Protein: 39g

GREEK LEG OF LAMB

(Prep time: 10 minutes\ Cook time: 8 hours\ 6 Servings)

Ingredients:

- 4 pound boneless lamb leg
- 1 tablespoon crushed rosemary
- 1 teaspoon freshly ground black pepper
- ¼ teaspoon kosher salt
- ¼ cup lemon juice
- ¼ cup water

Directions

1. Place lamb in slow cooker
2. Add remaining ingredients on top
3. Close the lid, and cook on LOW 8 hours
4. Remove the lamb, discard liquid, allow to rest 10 minutes before slicing

Nutrition Values (Per Serving)

- Calories: 350
- Fat: 21g
- Carbohydrates: 1g
- Protein: 38g

MOROCCAN LAMB STEW

(Prep time: 10 minutes\ Cook time: 8 hours \For 2 Servings)

Ingredients:

- ½ pound lean boneless lamb, cubed
- 2 cloves of garlic, minced
- ½ onion, chopped
- 2 tablespoons lemon juice
- ¼ cup sliced green olives
- 2 teaspoon date paste
- ¼ teaspoon turmeric
- 2 sprigs fresh thyme
- Pinch of salt, pepper

Directions

1. Place lamb, garlic, onion, lemon juice, olives, date paste, salt, pepper, turmeric to slow cooker
2. Top with sprigs of thyme
3. Cover with lid, and cook on LOW 8 hours
4. Serve in bowls over rice

Nutrition Values (Per Serving)

- Calories: 280
- Fat: 11g
- Carbohydrates: 13g
- Protein: 32g

LAMB STUFFED MEXICAN PEPPERS

(Prep time: 10 minutes\ Cook time: 5 hours\ 2 Servings)

Ingredients:

- 2 large poblano peppers, cut tops off, remove seeds
- 1 teaspoon olive oil
- 1 onion, diced
- 2 jalapenos, minced
- 4 cloves of garlic, minced
- 1 cup ground lamb
- 1 can (28 oz) crushed tomatoes

Directions

1. In a large skillet, heat olive oil, sauté onions, jalapenos, garlic, and meat until meat is no longer pink
2. Pour meat mixture in a medium bowl
3. Add half the can of tomatoes, stir well, fill the poblano peppers
4. Pour rest of the tomatoes along bottom of slow cooker
5. Place peppers standing up in slow cooker
6. Cover with lid, and cook on LOW 5 hours
7. Remove peppers from cooker, place on platter, drizzle sauce over peppers

Nutrition Values (Per Serving)

- Calories: 370
- Fat: 8g
- Carbohydrates: 52g
- Protein: 32g

RUSTIC LAMB STEW

(Prep time: 10 minutes\ Cook time: 4 hours\ 4 Servings)

Ingredients:

- 1½ pounds lamb stewing meat, 1-inch cubes
- ¼ cup almond flour
- 2 teaspoons olive oil
- ½ teaspoon thyme
- 1 teaspoon crushed rosemary
- 1 large onion, thinly sliced
- 2 cups water
- 1 cup baby carrots
- 1 cup potatoes, peeled, sliced
- 1 cup frozen peas
- Pinch of salt, pepper

Directions

1. In a bowl, season the flour with salt, pepper, rosemary. thyme
2. Season lamb with the flour
3. Heat olive oil in a deep skillet, sear lamb on all sides
4. Transfer to slow cooker, add potatoes, carrots
5. Reduce heat of skillet to medium, add onions, cook 4 minutes, until browned
6. Stir in water and deglaze skillet
7. Pour water and onion mixture over lamb chunks, potatoes, carrots
8. Cover with lid, and cook on LOW 4 hours
9. Add peas at the last minute
10. Serve on a platter

Nutrition Values (Per Serving)

- Calories: 387
- Fat: 11g
- Carbohydrates: 30g
- Protein: 39g

LEG OF LAMB WITH ROSEMARY

(Prep time: 20 minutes\ Cook time: 6-8 hours\ 4 Servings)

Ingredients:

- Olive oil
- 1 bone-in leg of lamb
- 4-5 Yukon potatoes, chopped in chunks
- 1 head of garlic, peeled
- Pinch of salt
- Few sprigs of rosemary
- ¼ cup red wine vinegar

Directions

1. Rub oil all over the lamb and brown it in a hot pan
2. Add potatoes and half of the garlic cloves to your cooker
3. Place lamb on top of the potatoes
4. Squish a few more cloves, rub over surface of leg
5. Season with salt
6. Add sprigs of rosemary and wine vinegar all around
7. Cover with lid, and cook on LOW 6 hours, check doneness, cook longer if needed
8. Remove lamb, serve with potatoes, add squeeze of lemon juice

Nutrition Values (Per Serving)

- Calories: 315
- Fat: 22g
- Carbohydrates: 2g
- Protein: 27g

GREEK LAMB AND POTATOES

(Prep time: 10 minutes\ Cook time: 6 hours\ 4-6 Servings)

Ingredients:

- 2 tablespoons olive oil
- 2½ pounds lamb shoulder
- 2 pounds baby potatoes
- 1 peeled and roughly chopped onion
- 3 crushed large garlic cloves
- 2 tablespoons lemon juice
- 1 teaspoon red wine vinegar
- 1 teaspoon anchovy paste
- ⅓ cup white wine vinegar
- ⅓ cup lamb broth
- 1 tablespoon dried oregano
- 1 cinnamon stick
- 1 tablespoon dried thyme
- Pinch of salt and pepper
- 1 lemon, divided in wedges
- Garnish: fresh oregano, fresh thyme

Directions

1. Season the lamb generously with salt and pepper
2. Rub with anchovy paste
3. Heat olive oil in a frying pan, and sear the lamb on all sides to brown it
4. Add potatoes, garlic, onion to pan, and fry 4 minutes
5. Transfer vegetables to slow cooker, place lamb on top
6. Add cinnamon stick and lemon wedges
7. Mix in vinegar, broth, lemon juice, herbs in the slow cooker
8. Cover with lid, and cook on LOW 6 hours
9. Once cooked, remove lamb, shred with 2 forks, serve with potatoes
10. Garnish with fresh oregano, fresh thyme, lemon wedges

Nutrition Values (Per Serving)

- Calories: 836
- Fat: 5g
- Carbohydrates: 10g
- Protein: 51g

CHAPTER 6: SEAFOOD RECIPES

SHRIMP CURRY

(Prep time: 5 minutes\ Cook time: 1 hour 20 minutes\ 4 Servings)

Ingredients:

- 1 pound shrimp, deveined
- 3 cups light coconut milk
- 1½ cups water
- ½ cup Thai red curry sauce
- 2½ teaspoons lemon garlic seasoning
- ¼ cup fresh cilantro

Directions

1. Add coconut milk, red curry sauce, lemon garlic ,water, seasoning to slow cooker
2. Stir well
3. Cover with lid, and cook on LOW 1 hour
4. Add shrimp, and cook 20 more minutes
5. Serve on platter, garnish with fresh cilantro

Nutrition Values (Per Serving)

- Calories: 576
- Fat: 22g
- Carbohydrates: 63g
- Protein: 32g

SALMON FILLET

(Prep time: 5 minutes\ Cook time: 1 hour\ 4 Servings)

Ingredients:

- 2 tablespoons ghee
- 1 small onion, thinly sliced
- 1 cup water
- 1 cup frozen vegetables
- 4 salmon fillets
- 1 tablespoon fresh lemon juice
- 1 sprig fresh dill
- Pinch of salt, pepper
- Garnish: lemon wedges, fresh dill

Directions

1. Grease slow cooker with ghee
2. Add onion slices, dill to cooker, pour in lemon juice, chicken broth, water
3. Cover with lid, and cook on HIGH 30 minutes
4. Remove lid, add fillets and frozen vegetables
5. Cover with lid, and cook on HIGH 30 minutes
6. Serve on platter, garnish with lemon wedges, fresh dill

Nutrition Values (Per Serving)

- Calories: 381
- Fat: 25g
- Carbohydrates: 4g
- Protein: 35g

TILAPIA AND ASPARAGUS

(Prep time: 20 minutes\ Cook time: 2 hours\ 4 Servings)

Ingredients:

- 12 asparagus, wood end removed
- 4-6 Tilapia Fillets
- 8-12 tablespoons lemon juice
- Pepper for seasoning
- Lemon juice for seasoning
- ½ tablespoon clarified butter for each fillet

Directions

1. Cut single pieces of foil for the fillets
2. Place piece of fillet on foil, season with pinch of pepper, squeeze of lemon juice
3. Drizzle clarified butter over fillet, top with 3 asparagus
4. Fold foil over the fish, and seal the ends
5. Transfer foil packets to slow cooker
6. Cover with lid, and cook on HIGH 2 hours
7. Serve hot

Nutrition Values (Per Serving)

- Calories: 229
- Fat: 10g
- Carbohydrates: 1g
- Protein: 28g

SHRIMP SCAMPI

(Prep time: 20 minutes\ Cook time: 2 hours\ 3 Servings)

Ingredients:

- ¼ cup chicken broth
- ½ cup white wine vinegar
- 2 tablespoons olive oil
- 2 teaspoons chopped garlic
- 2 teaspoons minced parsley
- 1 pound large, raw shrimp

Directions

1. Add all the ingredients to the slow cooker
2. Cover with lid, and cook on LOW 2 hours
3. Serve over rice, garnish with fresh parsley, lemon wedges

Nutrition Values (Per Serving)

- Calories: 293
- Fat: 24g
- Carbohydrates: 4g
- Protein: 16g

Spicy Seafood Stew

(Prep time: 20 minutes\ Cook time: 1 hour \For 8 Servings)

Ingredients:

- 1 tablespoon unsalted clarified butter
- 1 yellow onion, thinly sliced
- 2 garlic cloves, minced
- 2 celery stalks, chopped
- 1 fennel bulb, cored, thinly sliced
- 1 teaspoon dried oregano, 1 teaspoon fresh basil, 1 teaspoon fresh thyme
- 1 teaspoon cayenne pepper, 1 teaspoon red pepper flakes
- 1 cup white wine vinegar
- 1 can (28 oz) diced tomatoes
- 2 cups clam juice
- 1 pound littleneck clams, scrubbed
- 1 pound frozen crab
- 1 pound cod, 1-inch chunks
- ½ pound sea scallops
- 2 tablespoons fresh parsley

Directions

1. Soak clams in cold water as you prepare rest of ingredients
2. Set slow cooker to HIGH, add the ghee to melt it
3. Add onion, garlic sauté 5 minutes
4. Add fennel, oregano, celery, Chile, thyme and stir well
5. Add wine, tomatoes, broth and clam juice
6. Using a slotted spoon, transfer clams to slow cooker
7. Cover with lid, and cook on LOW 30 minutes
8. Using a slotted spoon, remove clams and discard
9. Add crab, close the lid, and cook on HIGH 15 minutes
10. Remove lid, add scallops and cod
11. Cover with lid, and cook 10 minutes
12. Serve on a platter, garnish with parsley, lemon wedges

Nutrition Values (Per Serving)

- Calories: 401
- Fat: 20g

- Carbohydrates: 9g
- Protein: 40g

FISH BROTH

(Prep time: 10 minutes\ Cook time: 8 hours\ 3 Servings)

Ingredients:

- 3 quarts water
- 2 onions, quartered
- Head of bones from 3 different fish
- 2 celery stalks, roughly chopped
- 2 tablespoon peppercorns
- Bunch of parsley
- 1 teaspoon salt and pepper, each

Directions

1. Add ingredients to slow cooker
2. Cover with lid, and cook on LOW 8 hours
3. Strain liquid, chill broth overnight
4. Skim any foam and use as needed

Nutrition Values (Per Serving)

- Calories: 401
- Fat: 20g
- Carbohydrates: 9g
- Protein: 40g

CLAM CHOWDER

(Prep time: 15 minutes\ Cook time: 3 hours\ 6 Servings)

Ingredients:

- 1 onion, diced
- 3 russet potatoes, peeled, diced
- 3 cans diced clams
- 1 cup clam juice
- ½ teaspoon dried clam juice
- ½ teaspoon dried thyme
- Pinch of salt, pepper
- 2 tablespoons ghee
- 3 tablespoons almond flour
- 1 cup almond milk
- 2 slices cooked bacon, crumbled or bacon bits

Directions

1. Add diced potatoes, onion to slow cooker
2. Stir in 2 cans of clams with the juice and 1 can without juice
3. Add (other) clam juice, salt, thyme, pepper and stir well
4. Cover with lid, and cook on HIGH 3 hours
5. After 3 hours, in a medium saucepan, melt the ghee over medium heat
6. Stir in flour, whisk in almond milk and stir until thickened
7. Whisk in the mixture slowly, to incorporate
8. Cook on HIGH until it thickens, 10 minutes approximately
9. Ladle into bowls, and top with crumbled bacon

Nutrition Values (Per Serving)

- Calories:43
- Fat: 20g
- Carbohydrates: 40g
- Protein: 27g

BBQ Shrimp

(Prep time: 10 minutes\ Cook time: 1 hour\ 4 Servings)

Ingredients:

- 2 pounds peeled, deveined shrimp
- 3 tablespoons ghee
- 3 tablespoons Whole30 Worcestershire sauce
- 2 teaspoons minced garlic
- 1 cup Whole30 BBQ sauce
- Pinch of salt, pepper
- Garnish: lemon wedges

Directions

1. Add shrimp to base of slow cooker
2. Add ghee, sauce, minced garlic, and BBQ sauce, stir well
3. Cover with lid, and cook on LOW 1 hour
4. Serve with rice, vegetables, garnish with lemon wedges

Nutrition Values (Per Serving)

- Calories: 241
- Fat: 15g
- Carbohydrates: 10g
- Protein: 18g

INDIAN FISH CURRY

(Prep time: 10 minutes\ Cook time: 2 hours\ 4 Servings)

Ingredients:

- ⅓ cup olive oil
- 1 yellow onion, finely chopped
- 2 garlic cloves, minced
- 2 small hot green chilies, seeded, minced
- 1 inch fresh ginger, peeled, grated
- 1 tablespoon cumin
- 2 teaspoons ground coriander
- 2 teaspoons brown mustard seeds
- 2 teaspoons ground turmeric
- 2 tomatoes, seeded, chopped
- 1 tablespoon curry paste
- Pinch of kosher salt
- 1½ cups water
- 2 pounds fish fillets; tilapia or cod, or your favorite choice – cut in 1-inch chunks
- 3 tablespoon fresh cilantro

Directions

1. Place the flame proof insert of slow cooker on stove element, heat to medium
2. Heat the olive oil, sauté onion, garlic 5 minutes
3. Add chilies, ginger, coriander, cumin, garlic, mustard, turmeric. Cook 5 more minutes
4. Add tomatoes, curry paste, salt. Cook 5 minutes
5. Add water, bring to a boil to deglaze the insert
6. Transfer insert to your slow cooker
7. Close with lid, and cook on PW 1 hour
8. Add fish, stirring gently to coat with sauce
9. Replace lid, and cook on LOW 30-45 minutes
10. Transfer to bowls, garnish with rice, fresh parsley

Nutrition Values (Per Serving)

- Calories: 368
- Fat: 27g
- Carbohydrates: 10g
- Protein: 26g

SPICY BBQ SHRIMP

(Prep time: 10 minutes\ Cook time: 1 hour\ 4 Servings)

Ingredients:

- 2 garlic cloves, minced
- 1 teaspoon Cajun seasoning
- ½ cup ghee
- ¼ cup Worcestershire sauce
- 1 tablespoon hot pepper sauce
- Juice from 1 lemon
- Pinch of salt and pepper
- 1½ pounds large, unpeeled shrimp
- 1 green onion, finely chopped

Directions

1. Add garlic, Cajun seasoning, ghee, sauce, hot pepper sauce, lemon juice, salt, pepper to slow cooker.
2. Cover with lid, and cook on HIGH 30 minutes
3. Rinse the shrimp and drain
4. Add shrimp to slow cooker, cover in sauce
5. Recover with lid, and cook on HIGH 30 minutes, until shrimp are cooked
6. Serve on platter, garnish with chopped green onion

Nutrition Values (Per Serving)

- Calories: 480
- Fat: 23g
- Carbohydrates: 35g
- Protein: 30g

Coconut Shrimp

(Prep time: 5 minutes\ Cook time: 1 hour, 30 minutes\ 4 Servings)

Ingredients:

- 1 pound shrimp, deveined, shelled
- 3 cups unsweetened coconut milk
- 2 cups water
- 1-2 tablespoons red curry paste
- 2½ teaspoons lemon garlic seasoning
- Garnish: fresh cilantro

Directions

1. Add coconut milk, water, lemon garlic, red curry sauce, seasoning to slow cooker
2. Stir well
3. Cover with lid, and cook on HIGH 1 hour
4. Remove cover, add shrimp, stir to coat evenly
5. Recover with lid, and cook 15-30 minutes, until shrimp is cooked
6. Serve on platter, garnish with cilantro

Nutrition Values (Per Serving)

- Calories: 351
- Fat: 12g
- Carbohydrates: 12g
- Protein: 14g

CHAPTER 7: POULTRY RECIPES

CHICKEN FAJITA LETTUCE WRAP

(Prep time: 20 minutes\ Cook time: 3 hours\ 4 Servings)

Ingredients

- 4 boneless, skinless chicken breasts
- 1½ teaspoon cumin
- ½ teaspoon smoked paprika
- 1 teaspoon sea salt
- Juice from 1 lime
- ½ cup green chilies, diced
- 1 cup salsa
- 1-2 tablespoons olive oil
- 1 small red bell pepper, sliced
- 1 small red onion, diced
- 1 small yellow onion, sliced
- Large leaves of lettuce for tortilla wraps

Directions

1. Place chicken breasts in slow cooker
2. Add paprika, chili powder, cumin, salt, lime juice. Stir well
3. Add Salsa and green chilies. Stir
4. Cover with lid, and cook 3 hours until chicken is no longer pink in middle
5. As the 3 hour mark approaches, in a large skillet, heat olive oil. Sauté sliced red pepper, onions until brown
6. Remove chicken, shred using 2 forks. Return to cooker. Simmer 10 minutes
7. Serve over lettuce wraps

Nutrition Values (Per Serving)

- Calories: 315
- Fat: 52g
- Carbohydrates: 25g
- Protein: 32g

CHICKEN CURRY

(Prep time: 10 minutes\ Cook time: 6 hours\ 4 Servings)

Ingredients

- 1 tablespoon olive oil
- 1 cup chopped leeks
- 2 garlic cloves, minced
- 1½ tablespoons curry powder
- 1 cup almond milk
- ½ cup water
- 8 boneless, skinless chicken thighs
- 3 celery stalks, diced
- Garnish: toasted slivered almonds, diced green onions

Directions

1. In a small skillet heat the olive oil
2. Sauté the leeks, garlic until tender
3. Transfer to slow cooker
4. Add rest of listed ingredients, excluding almonds
5. Cover with lid, cook on LOW 6 hours
6. Serve over rice, garnish with slivered almonds, green onions

Nutrition Values (Per Serving)

- Calories: 1222
- Fat: 98g
- Carbohydrates: 24g
- Protein: 67g

PINEAPPLE CHICKEN

(Prep time: 20 minutes\ Cook time: 4 hours 30 minutes\ 8 Servings)

Ingredients

- 1 cup (canned) pineapple chunks
- 7 tablespoons red curry paste
- 3 tablespoons fish sauce
- 2 teaspoons fresh lime juice
- 2 teaspoons fresh grated ginger
- 2 teaspoons curry paste
- 1 small white onion, sliced
- 6 chicken breasts, diced in 1-inch chunks
- ½ cup coconut milk
- 1 small red pepper, sliced
- Garnish: fresh cilantro, sesame seeds

Directions

1. In a bowl, combine pineapple juice, fish sauce, ginger, lime juice, curry paste
2. Place sliced onion along bottom of slow cooker
3. Place chicken over the onion
4. Pour sauce over the chicken
5. Cover with lid, and cook on LOW 4 hours
6. After 4 hours, remove lid, add coconut milk, bell pepper, pineapple chunks, stir
7. Recover with lid, and cook 30 more minutes
8. Serve over rice or noodles, garnish with sesame seeds, fresh cilantro

Nutrition Values (Per Serving)

- Calories: 254
- Fat: 24g
- Carbohydrates: 43g
- Protein: 23g

GARLIC AND ONION TURKEY

(Prep time: 10 minutes\ Cook time: 6 hours\ 8 Servings)

Ingredients

- 5 large onions, thinly sliced
- 4 garlic cloves, minced
- ¼ cup white wine
- ½ teaspoon sea salt
- ¼ teaspoon black pepper
- ¼ teaspoon cayenne pepper
- 4 large skinless turkey thighs

Directions

1. Place onion, garlic along bottom of slow cooker
2. Pour in white wine, cayenne pepper, salt, black pepper
3. Place turkey thighs over ingredients
4. Cover with lid, and cook on LOW 6 hours
5. Remove the turkey from the crock pot, remove meat from bones
6. Return to slow cooker, simmer in the liquid 5 minutes
7. Serve on a platter

Nutrition Values (Per Serving)

- Calories: 845
- Fat: 41g
- Carbohydrates: 7g
- Protein: 107g

BOLOGNESE TURKEY SAUCE

(Prep time: 10 minutes\ Cook time: 4 hours\ 4 Servings)

Ingredients:

- 1 can (28 oz) organic tomato sauce/puree
- 1 can (8 oz) organic tomato paste
- ½ cup chicken broth
- 1 tablespoon olive oil
- 2 teaspoons Italian herbs blend
- 1 teaspoon sea salt
- ½ teaspoon black pepper
- Pinch of crushed red pepper flakes
- 3 garlic cloves, minced
- 2 small carrots, diced
- 1 small onion, diced
- 1 pound lean ground turkey
- Garnish: fresh parsley, parmesan cheese

Directions

1. Heat slow cooker to high
2. Heat up olive oil, sauté onion, garlic, carrots 5 minutes
3. Add ground turkey, italian herbs, salt, pepper, crushed red peppers. Stir well
4. Add tomato paste, tomato sauce, chicken broth. Stir well
5. Cover with lid, and cook on LOW 4 hours
6. Serve over pasta, garnish with fresh parsley, parmesan cheese

Nutrition Values (Per Serving)

- Calories: 219
- Fat: 3g
- Carbohydrates: 33g
- Protein: 13g

TIKKA MASALA

(Prep time: 15 minutes\ Cook time: 4 hours\ 6 Servings)

Ingredients

- 2 tablespoons olive oil
- 6 chicken thighs, diced in 1-inch pieces
- 1 yellow onion, diced
- 2 garlic cloves, minced
- 2 teaspoons coarse salt
- 1½ tablespoons Garam masala
- ½ teaspoon paprika
- 3 tablespoons tomato paste
- 1 can (28 oz) diced tomatoes
- 1 can (15 oz) coconut milk
- Garnish: fresh cilantro

Directions

1. In a skillet over medium temp, heat olive oil
2. Sauté onion, garlic 5 minutes
3. Season chicken with salt and pepper, sear chicken on all sides
4. Transfer all to slow cooker
5. Add diced tomatoes, tomato paste, garam masala, paprika. Stir well
6. Cover with lid, and cook on HIGH 4 hours
7. Once cooked, open lid and simmer 30 minutes if you want a thick sauce
8. Serve on a platter, garnish with fresh cilantro, side with naan bread

Nutrition Values (Per Serving)

- Calories: 421
- Fat: 15g
- Carbohydrates: 47g
- Protein: 52g

CHICKEN TERIYAKI

(Prep time: 10 minutes\ Cook time: 4 hours\ 6 Servings)

Ingredients:

- 2 pounds chicken drumsticks
- ½ cup Whole30 Teriyaki Sauce
- Pinch of salt, pepper
- Garnish: sesame seeds

Preparation:

1. Season drumsticks with salt and pepper
2. Place in slow cooker
3. Pour sauce over drumsticks
4. Cover with lid, and cook on LOW 4 hours
5. Remove meat, and transfer to oven safe dish
6. Broil few minutes per side
7. Garnish with sesame seeds

Nutrition Values (Per Serving)

- Calories: 430
- Fat: 8g
- Carbohydrates: 71g
- Protein: 22g

INDIAN CHICKEN SAAG

(Prep time: 5 minutes\ Cook time: 4 hours\ 8 Servings)

Ingredients:

- 4-5 garlic cloves, finely chopped
- 3-inch fresh ginger, grated
- 1 x 15 oz can organic tomato sauce
- 1 tablespoon Garam Masala
- 1 tablespoon ground coriander
- 1 tablespoon ground cumin
- Pinch of salt
- Pinch or two cayenne pepper
- 1 x 13.5 oz can full fat coconut milk
- 2 x 16 oz bags fresh spinach
- 1½ pounds boneless, skinless chicken breast, cubed in bite-sized pieces
- Garnish: fresh cilantro

Preparation:

1. Add garlic, ginger, tomato paste, garam marsala, coriander, cumin, salt, cayenne pepper, coconut milk, spinach to slow cooker
2. Cover with lid, and cook on LOW 3 hours
3. After 2 and a half hours, pulse ingredients with immersion blender
4. Add cubed chicken to slow cooker
5. Recover with lid, and cook 1 more hour
6. Serve over cauliflower rice, garnish with fresh cilantro

Nutrition Values (Per Serving)

- Calories: 290
- Fat: 10g
- Carbohydrates: 35g
- Protein: 19g

LEMON AND THYME CHICKEN

(Prep time: 10 minutes\ Cook time: 6-8 hours\ 4 Servings)

Ingredients:

- 4 pound whole chicken
- ¼ cup fresh squeeze lemon juice
- 1 teaspoon dried thyme
- 3 bay leaves
- 4 garlic cloves, diced
- Pinch of salt, pepper

Directions

1. Remove giblets from inside chicken, rinse chicken under cool water
2. Place chicken in slow cooker
3. Drizzle lemon juice over chicken, season with salt, pepper, thyme
4. Place bay leaves, garlic cloves around the chicken
5. Cover with lid, and cook on LOW 6-8 hours (check after 6 hours, and every 30 minutes until it reaches internal temperature for chicken on cooking thermometer)

Nutrition Values (Per Serving)

- Calories: 490
- Fat: 16g
- Carbohydrates: 39g
- Protein: 45g

MEXICAN TURKEY CASSEROLE

(Prep time: 5 minutes\ Cook time: 4 hours\ 6 Servings)

Ingredients:

- 4 sweet potato, peeled, cubed
- 8 eggs, whisked
- ½ pound cooked turkey bacon, crumbled
- 1 yellow onion, chopped
- 1 red bell pepper, chopped
- 1 pack mushrooms, chopped
- ½ pack taco seasoning (Whole30 approved)
- Garnish: guacamole, jalapeno, salsa

Directions

1. Cook the bacon, pull from pan, crumble
2. Add onion, bell peppers to pan. Sauté 5 minutes
3. Transfer to slow cooker
4. Add taco seasoning, eggs, mushrooms. Stir
5. Cover with lid, and cook on LOW 4 hours
6. Serve on a platter with jalapeno, salsa, guacamole

Nutrition Values (Per Serving)

- Calories: 308
- Fat: 18g
- Carbohydrates: 21g
- Protein: 15g

TINGA CHICKEN

(Prep time: 10 minutes\ Cook time: 4 hours\ 6 Servings)

Ingredients:

- 2 pounds boneless, skinless chicken breast
- 1 large onion, minced
- 4 garlic cloves, minced
- 1½ cup diced tomatoes and green chilies
- 3 tablespoons chipotle peppers
- ½ teaspoon salt

Directions

1. Add listed ingredients to slow cooker, except tomatoes
2. Mix well
3. Cover with lid, and cook on HIGH 4 hours
4. Remove the chicken, shred it
5. Return chicken to slow cooker, add tomatoes
6. Cook another 30 minutes
7. Serve on a platter over cauliflower rice, or noodles, garnish with fresh parsley

Nutrition Values (Per Serving)

- Calories: 190
- Fat: 6g
- Carbohydrates: 3g
- Protein: 30g

Sweet And Sour Chicken

(Prep time: 10 minutes\ Cook time: 6 hours, 30 minutes\ 4 Servings)

Ingredients:

- 1 pound boneless, skinless chicken breasts, diced in bite-size pieces
- ½ cup sweet and sour sauce
- ¼ teaspoon garlic powder
- ¼ teaspoon onion powder
- 1 cup pineapple chunks (¼ cup of juice reserved)
- 1 tablespoon date paste
- 2 cups frozen vegetables

Directions

1. Spray slow cooker with non-stick spray
2. Add chicken, onion, garlic powder to slow cooker. Stir
3. Stir in sweet and sour sauce, pineapple chunks, and the ¼ cup pineapple juice
4. Cover with lid, and cook on LOW 6 hours
5. Add frozen vegetables during final 30 minutes

Nutrition Values (Per Serving)

- Calories: 206
- Fat: 3g
- Carbohydrates: 19g
- Protein: 25g

ARTICHOKE AND CHICKEN

(Prep time: 10 minutes\ Cook time: 8 hours\ 6 Servings)

Ingredients:

- 1 pound, boneless, skinless chicken breasts
- 1 pound boneless, skinless chicken thighs
- 1 can (14 oz) canned artichoke hearts packed in water, drained
- 1 onion, diced
- 2 carrots, diced
- 2 celery stalks, diced
- 3 garlic cloves, minced
- 1 bay leaf
- ½ teaspoon black pepper
- 3 cups peeled, cubed turnips
- 6 cups vegetable broth
- ¼ cup fresh squeezed lemon juice
- ¼ cup fresh parsley

Directions

1. Add listed ingredients to slow cooker, except parsley and lemon juice
2. Cover with lid, and cook on LOW 8 hours
3. Remove the chicken, shred it
4. Return chicken to slow cooker, add lemon juice, salt, pepper
5. Simmer 5 minutes
6. Serve on a platter, garnish with fresh parsley

Nutrition Values (Per Serving)

- Calories: 400
- Fat: 10g
- Carbohydrates: 12g
- Protein: 3g

CREAMY CHICKEN

(Prep time: 5 minutes\ Cook time: 6 hours\ 4 Servings)

Ingredients:

- 1 cup chicken broth
- 1 green bell pepper, sliced
- 1 red bell pepper, sliced
- 1 thinly sliced carrot
- 1 cup Almond milk
- 3 cups boneless, skinless chicken breasts, diced
- 1½ cups water
- Garnish: fresh parsley

Directions

1. Grease slow cooker with non-stick spray
2. Add listed ingredients to slow cooker
3. Cover with lid, and cook on LOW 6 hours
4. Serve in bowls over rice, garnish with fresh parsley

Nutrition Values (Per Serving)

- Calories: 269
- Fat: 20g
- Carbohydrates: 8g
- Protein: 13g

Chapter 8: Salad Recipes

Warm Veggie Medley
(Prep time: 5 minutes\ Cook time: 3 hours\ 6 Servings)

Ingredients

- 2 cups Okra, sliced
- 2 cups grape tomatoes
- 1 red onion, diced
- 2 yellow bell peppers, sliced
- 2 medium Zucchini, sliced
- 1 cup sliced mushrooms
- ½ cup Balsamic vinegar
- ½ cup olive oil
- 2 tablespoons fresh basil
- 1 tablespoon fresh thyme
- Garnish: fresh basil leaves

Directions

1. In a bowl, combine balsamic vinegar, olive oil, salt, pepper, basil, thyme
2. Whisk until combined
3. Add veggies to slow cooker. Pour in marinade. Stir
4. Cover with lid, and cook on HIGH 3 hours
5. Serve on platter, garnish with fresh basil

Nutrition Values (Per Serving)

- Calories: 233
- Fat: 18g
- Carbohydrates: 14g
- Protein: 3g

Vegetable Chili Salad

(Prep time: 10 minutes\ Cook time: 5 hours\ 6 Servings)

Ingredients

- 2 tablespoons olive oil
- 2 white onions, finely chopped
- 2 garlic cloves, minced
- 1 red bell pepper, finely sliced
- 1 yellow bell pepper, finely sliced
- 2 cans diced tomatoes
- 1 cup vegetable broth
- 2 cans red kidney beans
- 1 cup salsa sauce
- 1 teaspoon paprika
- 1 teaspoon salt, pepper
- Garnish: fresh parsley

Directions

1. In a large skillet, heat the olive oil
2. Sauté garlic, onions, yellow pepper, red pepper
3. Transfer to slow cooker
4. Add tomatoes, kidney beans, salsa, broth
5. Season with salt, pepper, paprika. Stir
6. Cover with lid, and cook on LOW 5 hours
7. Serve in bowls, garnish with fresh parsley

Nutrition Values (Per Serving)

- Calories: 181
- Fat: 15g
- Carbohydrates: 10g
- Protein: 6g

Eggplant Salad

(Prep time: 10 minutes\ Cook time: 4 hours\ 6 Servings)

Ingredients

- 1 red onion, sliced
- 2 red bell peppers, diced
- 1 large eggplant, sliced and quartered
- 1 can (24 oz) whole tomatoes
- 1 tablespoon smoked paprika
- 2 teaspoons smoked cumin
- Pinch of black pepper
- Juice from 1 lemon

Directions

1. Add listed ingredients to slow cooker. Stir
2. Cover with lid, and cook on LOW 4 hours
3. Serve over cauliflower rice

Nutrition Values (Per Serving)

- Calories: 290
- Fat: 8g
- Carbohydrates: 51g
- Protein: 6g

German Potato Salad

(Prep time: 30 minutes\ Cook time: 2 hours\ 12 Servings)

Ingredients

- ½ pound chopped bacon
- 1¼ cup chopped onion
- 1¼ cup chopped celery
- 1½ teaspoon salt
- ¾ teaspoon celery seed
- ½ teaspoon pepper
- 2 pounds small red potatoes
- 1 cup chicken broth
- 2 tablespoons arrowroot
- ¼ cup cider vinegar
- 2 tablespoons fresh parsley

Directions

1. Cook the bacon, pull from pan, crumble
2. In the same pan, cook onion, celery 5 minutes
3. Place potatoes in slow cooker, pour in onion, celery mix
4. Pour in broth, season with salt, pepper, celery seeds
5. Cover with lid, and cook on LOW 2 hours (continue cooking if not done)
6. Combine arrowroot and vinegar in a small bowl
7. Pour liquid in slow cooker, add crumbled bacon
8. Cook on HIGH 5 minutes
9. Serve in a bowl, garnish with fresh parsley

Nutrition Values (Per Serving)

- Calories: 130
- Fat: 3g
- Carbohydrates: 22g
- Protein: 4g

CHICKEN SALAD

(Prep time: 10 minutes\ Cook time: 3 hours\ 8 Servings)

Ingredients

- 2 pounds boneless, skinless chicken breast
- ½ small onion, diced
- 2 celery stalks, diced
- ½ cup chicken broth
- 1½ cups Whole30 mayo
- ½ cup seedless grapes
- ½ cup chopped pecans
- ¼ teaspoon salt
- ¼ teaspoon pepper
- Garnish: fresh dill

Directions

1. Add chicken, onion, celery, broth to slow cooker
2. Cover with lid, and cook on LOW 3 hours, until thoroughly cooked
3. Shred the chicken using a fork, allow to cool
4. In a bowl, combine chicken, grapes, salt, pepper, pecans, mayo. Stir
5. Garnish with fresh dill

Nutrition Values (Per Serving)

- Calories: 130
- Fat: 3g
- Carbohydrates: 22g
- Protein: 4g

CHAPTER 9: SIDE DISHES RECIPES

CABBAGE CASSEROLE

(Prep time: 10 minutes\ Cook time: 4 hours\ 4 Servings)

Ingredients

- ½ cabbage, roughly sliced
- 1 onion, diced
- 3 garlic cloves, finely chopped
- 1½ cups crushed tomatoes
- 2 cups cauliflower rice
- 4 tablespoons ghee
- 1 heaping tablespoon Italian Seasoning
- ½ teaspoon crushed red pepper
- Pinch of salt, pepper
- Garnish: fresh parsley

Directions

1. Add listed ingredients to slow cooker, except the parsley
2. Cover with lid, and cook on LOW 4 hours
3. Serve in a bowl, garnish with parsley

Nutrition Values (Per Serving)

- Calories: 320
- Fat: 18g
- Carbohydrates: 0g
- Protein: 17g

SQUASH AND MANGO MEDLEY

(Prep time: 10 minutes\ Cook time: 3 hours\ 4 Servings)

Ingredients

- 1 large acorn squash, peeled, deseeded, diced
- ¼ cup mango chutney
- ¼ cup flaked coconut
- Pinch of salt, pepper

Directions

1. Grease slow cooker with olive oil
2. Place squash in slow cooker
3. In a bowl, combine coconut, chutney, pour over squash
4. Season with salt, pepper
5. Cover with lid, and cook on LOW 3 hours
6. Serve in a bowl

Nutrition Values (Per Serving)

- Calories: 226
- Fat: 6g
- Carbohydrates: 24g
- Protein: 17g

Dijon Potato Salad

(Prep time: 15 minutes\ Cook time: 2 hours\ 4 Servings)

Ingredients

- 1-2 tablespoons Dijon mustard
- 1 tablespoon olive oil
- 2 tablespoons red wine vinegar
- Pinch of salt, pepper
- 1 teaspoon dried rosemary
- 6 medium potatoes, peeled, cubed
- ¼ cup beef, chicken, or vegetable broth
- 1 small red onion, diced
- Garnish: fresh parsley

Directions

1. Grease slow cooker with olive oil
2. Place potatoes, diced onion in slow cooker
3. Pour in broth. Season with salt, pepper
4. Cover with lid, and cook on LOW 2 hours
5. In a bowl, combine Dijon mustard, red wine vinegar, rosemary. Whisk until combined
6. Cool the potatoes slightly before pouring vinaigrette over potatoes
7. Serve in a bowl, garnish with fresh parsley

Nutrition Values (Per Serving)

- Calories: 196
- Fat: 4g
- Carbohydrates: 37g
- Protein: 4g

MASHED CAULIFLOWER

(Prep time: 5 minutes\ Cook time: 2 hours\ 4 Servings)

Ingredients

- 1 large cauliflower, diced in florets
- 6 garlic cloves, peeled, minced
- 4 tablespoons herbs; rosemary, parsley, chives
- 1 cup vegetable broth
- 4-6 cups water
- 3 tablespoons melted ghee
- Pinch of salt, pepper

Directions

1. Place cauliflower florets, garlic cloves, vegetable broth, and enough water to cover cauliflower in slow cooker
2. Cover with lid, and cook on LOW 2 hours
3. Drain liquid, return cauliflower to slow cooker
4. Add ghee, salt, pepper
5. Mash until desired consistency
6. Serve in a bowl, garnish with rosemary, parsley, chives

Nutrition Values (Per Serving)

- Calories: 25
- Fat: 5g
- Carbohydrates: 0g
- Protein: 2g

BAKED POTATOES

(Prep time: 5 minutes\ Cook time: 2 hours\ 4 Servings)

Ingredients

- 6 russet potatoes
- ½ cup water

Directions

1. Wash the potatoes, pierce the potatoes in a few places, wrap in aluminum foil
2. Pour water in slow cooker, place potatoes in slow cooker
3. Cover with lid, and cook on LOW 2 hours, until fork tender
4. Remove from slow cooker, transfer to serving platter

Nutrition Values (Per Serving)

- Calories: 170
- Fat:0g
- Carbohydrates: 33g
- Protein: 5g

POTATO HASH

(Prep time: 10 minutes\ Cook time: 2 hours\ 2 Servings)

Ingredients:

- 1 medium orange pepper, diced
- 1 medium yellow pepper, diced
- ¼ cup butternut squash, peeled, deseeded, diced
- 4 sweet potatoes, peeled, diced
- 2 medium tomatoes, thinly diced
- 1 small onion, diced
- 1 tablespoon coconut oil
- 1 teaspoon garlic puree
- 1 teaspoon thyme
- 1 teaspoon mustard powder
- Pinch of salt, pepper

Directions

1. Place all the vegetables in slow cooker
2. Season with onion, garlic puree, thyme, mustard powder
3. Add coconut oil to slow cooker
4. Mix well
5. Cover with lid, and cook on LOW 2 hours, until fork tender
6. Transfer to serving platter, mash slightly

Nutrition Values (Per Serving)

- Calories: 270
- Fat: 10g
- Carbohydrates: 39g
- Protein: 5g

LIVER PATE

(Prep time: 5 minutes\ Cook time: 3 hours\ 16 Servings)

Ingredients

- 1 pound chicken livers
- ¼ cup finely chopped red onion
- ½ cup clarified butter at room temperature
- ½ teaspoon of paprika
- ½ teaspoon of ground black pepper
- Pinch of salt

Directions

1. Add listed ingredients to slow cooker
2. Cover with lid, and cook on HIGH 3 hours
3. Transfer mixture to food processor, puree until creamy texture forms
4. Refrigerate unused portion

Nutrition Values (Per Serving)

- Calories: 308
- Fat: 24g
- Carbohydrates: 2g
- Protein: 16g

GREEN CURRY WINGS

(Prep time: 10 minutes\ Cook time: 4 hours\ 10 Servings)

Ingredients

- 3 pounds chicken wings
- 1 cup green curry paste
- 2 tablespoons Thai basil, minced
- 1 tablespoon coconut milk
- 1 tablespoon minced fresh ginger
- 1 tablespoon fresh cilantro
- 2 tablespoons water

Directions

1. In a small bowl, combine curry paste, basil, coconut milk, cilantro, ginger. Whisk until combined
2. Add wings to slow cooker
3. Pour sauce over wings, stir to coat
4. Cover with lid, and cook on LOW 4 hours
5. Serve on platter, garnish with fresh parsley

Nutrition Values (Per Serving)

- Calories: 320
- Fat: 23g
- Carbohydrates: 1g
- Protein: 26g

CARAMELIZED ONIONS

(Prep time: 10 minutes\ Cook time: 3 hours\ 1 quart)

Ingredients

- 4 pounds sweet onion, peeled, separate onions into rings
- 3 tablespoons ghee
- 1 tablespoon balsamic vinegar

Directions

1. Place onions rings in slow cooker
2. Combine ghee and balsamic vinegar in a bowl, whisk
3. Drizzle over onions
4. Cover with lid, and cook on LOW 3 hours
5. If the onions are properly caramelized, pour on serving platter
6. If not, turn slow cooker to HIGH, and cook 30 more minutes

Nutrition Values (Per Serving)

- Calories: 35
- Fat: 1g
- Carbohydrates: 6g
- Protein: 1g

EGGPLANT BABA GANOUSH

(Prep time: 10 minutes\ Cook time: 2 hours\ 5 Servings)

Ingredients

- 1 pound eggplant
- 2 tablespoons tahini
- 2 tablespoons lemon juice
- 2 garlic cloves, minced
- Garnish: fresh dill

Directions

1. Pierce eggplant with fork
2. Place in slow cooker
3. Cover with lid, and cook on HIGH 2 hours
4. Remove from slow cooker, allow to cool
5. Peel the skin, slice in half and deseed
6. Place in a bowl, add tahini, lemon juice, garlic cloves. Mash to desired consistency
7. Garnish with fresh dill

Nutrition Values (Per Serving)

- Calories: 25
- Fat: 2g
- Carbohydrates: 3g
- Protein: 1g

SALSA

(Prep time: 10 minutes\ Cook time: 2 hours\ 10 Servings)

Ingredients

- 4 cups grape tomatoes, halved
- 1 small onion, thinly sliced
- 2 jalapenos, diced
- small bunch of cilantro for cooking process
- Pinch of salt, pepper
- Garnish: fresh cilantro

Directions

1. Add ingredients to slow cooker
2. Stir well
3. Cover with lid, and cook on LOW 2 hours
4. Transfer to bowl, allow to cool completely
5. Season if necessary, garnish with fresh cilantro

Nutrition Values (Per Serving)

- Calories: 20
- Fat: 0g
- Carbohydrates: 4g
- Protein: 1g

CHAPTER 10: SOUPS, BROTH, AND STEWS RECIPES

TOMATO AND SPINACH SOUP

(Prep time: 5 minutes\ Cook time: 3 hours\ 2 Servings)

Ingredients

- 1 cup baby spinach
- 2 medium carrots, chopped
- 2 celery stalks, chopped
- 1 large onion, chopped
- 1 garlic clove, minced
- 4 cups low sodium vegetable broth
- 1 can (28 oz) diced tomatoes
- 2 bay leaves
- 1 tablespoon dried basil
- 1 teaspoon dried oregano
- ½ teaspoon crushed red pepper flakes
- Garnish: baked toast, fresh parsley

Directions

1. Add listed ingredients to slow cooker
2. Cover with lid, and cook on LOW 3 hours
3. Open the lid, remove bay leaves
4. Serve in bowls, garnish with baked toast, fresh parsley

Nutrition Values (Per Serving)

- Calories: 98
- Fat: 2g
- Carbohydrates: 16g
- Protein: 5g

BUTTERNUT SQUASH SOUP

(Prep time: 15 minutes\ Cook time: 3 hours\ 6 Servings)

Ingredients

- 1 onion, chopped
- 3 large carrots, peeled, chopped
- 3 garlic cloves, minced
- 1 large butternut squash, peeled, deseeded, chopped
- 4 cups vegetable broth
- Garnish: fresh ground black pepper, cream

Directions

1. Add listed ingredients to slow cooker
2. Cover with lid, cook on LOW 3 hours, until squash fork tender
3. Using an immersion blender, blend to desired consistency
4. Serve in bowls, garnish with pepper, cream

Nutrition Values (Per Serving)

- Calories: 100
- Fat: 2.5g
- Carbohydrates: 20g
- Protein: 2g

RUSTIC TOMATO SOUP

(Prep time: 5 minutes\ Cook time: 4 hours\ 6 Servings)

Ingredients

- 2 large carrots, peeled, chopped
- 2 large celery stalks, diced
- 1 onion, chopped
- 4 garlic cloves, minced
- 6 cups (3 large cans) whole tomatoes with juice
- 2 cups roasted red peppers in water
- 4 cups vegetable broth
- ¼ cup fresh basil
- 1 bay leaf
- Pinch of salt, pepper
- Garnish: baked toast, grated cheese, fresh ground black pepper

Directions

1. Add ingredients to slow cooker
2. Cover with lid, and cook on LOW 4 hours
3. Remove lid, blend using immersion blender to desired consistency
4. Pour in bowls, season with baked toast, grated cheese, fresh ground black pepper

Nutrition Values (Per Serving)

- Calories: 100
- Fat: 2g
- Carbohydrates: 16g
- Protein: 5g

CREAMY CARROT SOUP

Prep time: 20 minutes\ Cook time: 4 hours\ 6 Servings)

Ingredients

- 8 medium carrots, peeled, diced
- 1 onion, chopped
- 1 apple, peeled, chopped
- 1 garlic clove, crushed
- 1 teaspoon curry powder
- ¼ teaspoon salt
- Pinch of allspice
- 3 cups vegetable broth
- 1 cup almond milk
- Garnish: fresh cilantro, cream, fresh ground black pepper

Directions

1. Add carrots, onion, apple, onion, garlic, curry powder, salt, broth, allspice to slow cooker
2. Cover with lid, and cook LOW 4 hours, until carrots are tender
3. Using an immersion blender, blend to desired consistency, smooth
4. Stir in almond milk, simmer 5 minutes on HIGH
5. Ladle into bowls, garnish with fresh cilantro, cream, fresh ground black pepper

Nutrition Values (Per Serving)

- Calories: 98
- Fat: 2g
- Carbohydrates: 16g
- Protein: 5g

HEARTY VEGETABLE SOUP

(Prep time: 15 minutes\ Cook time: 2-4 hours\ 6 Servings)

Ingredients

- 1-2 tablespoons olive oil
- 1 medium yellow onion, chopped
- 2 cups mushrooms, sliced, your choice
- 1 large green bell pepper, chopped
- 1 large yellow bell pepper, chopped
- 1 tablespoon garlic powder, 1 tablespoon dried parsley, 1 tablespoon dried thyme
- 2 tablespoon of dried marjoram
- 1 teaspoon of celery seed, 1 teaspoon dried rosemary
- 2 teaspoons dried basil
- 2 medium zucchini, chopped
- 6 cups vegetable broth
- Pinch of salt, pepper

Directions

1. In a large skillet, heat the olive oil
2. Sauté onion, mushrooms, green and yellow peppers 5 minutes
3. Transfer to slow cooker
4. Add zucchini, broth, spices to slow cooker
5. Cover with lid, and cook on LOW 2-4 hours
6. Ladle in bowls, garnish with cilantro

Nutrition Values (Per Serving)

- Calories: 100
- Fat: 2.5g
- Carbohydrates: 20g
- Protein: 2g

VENISON CHILI

(Prep time: 20 minutes\ Cook time: 3 hours\ 6 Servings)

Ingredients:

- 2 pounds ground venison
- 1 medium yellow onion, diced
- 4 garlic cloves, crushed
- 1 cup red kidney beans
- 1 red bell pepper, diced
- 1 orange bell pepper, diced
- 1 cup shredded cabbage
- 1 can (28 oz) diced tomatoes
- 1 can (14 oz) tomato sauce
- 2 tablespoons clarified butter
- 2 teaspoons chili powder
- 1 teaspoon ground cumin
- ½ teaspoon paprika
- ½ teaspoon cayenne pepper
- Garnish: minced cashews, fresh cilantro

Directions

1. In a medium pan, melt the butter
2. Sauté onion, garlic, venison meat until meat browned
3. Transfer to slow cooker, along with remaining ingredients
4. Cover with lid, and cook on LOW 3 hours
5. Ladle into bowls, garnish with cashews, fresh cilantro

Nutrition Values (Per Serving)

- Calories: 300
- Fat: 10g
- Carbohydrates: 29g
- Protein: 26g

FAJITA SOUP

(Prep time: 10 minutes\ Cook time: 3 hours\ 4 Servings)

Ingredients:

- 6 cups chicken broth
- 1 large tomato, diced
- 1 zucchini, diced
- 1 small chinese eggplant, cubed
- 1 small onion, diced
- 1 pound yellow green beans, diced
- 2 chicken breasts, cubed
- 2 tablespoons Fajita seasoning
- 1 tablespoon lime juice
- Garnish: fresh parsley, tortilla strips

Directions

1. Add listed ingredients to slow cooker
2. Cover with lid, and cook on LOW 3 hours
3. Ladle into bowls, garnish with fresh cilantro, tortilla strips

Nutrition Values (Per Serving)

- Calories: 90
- Fat: 3g
- Carbohydrates: 13g
- Protein: 8g

TOM-KHA-YUM SOUP

(Prep time: 10 minutes\ Cook time: 4 hours\ 4 Servings)

Ingredients:

- 1 pound chicken tenders, diced
- 2 large cans full-fat coconut milk
- 2 cups chicken broth
- 2 larges cans (2x 28 oz) diced tomatoes
- 1 small sweet onion
- 2 tablespoons red curry paste
- 2 inch ginger, peeled, grated
- 2 tablespoons fish sauce
- 2 tablespoons lime juice
- 2 cups sliced mushrooms
- Garnish: fresh cilantro

Directions

1. Add chicken along bottom of slow cooker
2. Add rest of ingredients, except mushrooms and cilantro
3. Cover with lid, and cook on LOW 4 hours
4. Add mushrooms 20 minutes before end of cooking
5. Serve in bowls, garnish with cilantro

Nutrition Values (Per Serving)

- Calories: 357
- Fat: 25g
- Carbohydrates: 0g
- Protein: 29g

ZUPPA TOSCANA

(Prep time: 5 minutes\ Cook time: 2 hours\ 4 Servings)

Ingredients:

- 4 slices Whole30 compliant bacon, diced
- 1 pound lean Italian sausage
- ½ teaspoon crushed red pepper flakes
- 4 medium yellow potatoes, diced
- 1 onion, diced
- 2 tablespoons minced garlic
- 4 cups chicken broth
- ½ bunch of kale
- 1 can coconut milk
- Pinch of salt, pepper

Directions

1. Set your slow cooker to HIGH, add Italian sausage
2. Sprinkle in red pepper flakes
3. Add the bacon, cook 5 minutes, until crisp
4. Remove the bacon, set aside
5. Stir in garlic, onion, and cook 5 minutes
6. Pour in chicken broth
7. Add potatoes
8. Cover with lid, and cook on LOW 2 hours
9. Add bacon and kale to soup, stir in coconut milk
10. Season with salt and pepper
11. Serve in bowls, garnish with fresh parsley

Nutrition Values (Per Serving)

- Calories: 50
- Fat: 4g
- Carbohydrates: 0g
- Protein: 0g

THAI TURKEY SOUP

(Prep time: 10 minutes\ Cook time: 2 hours\ 4 Servings)

Ingredients:

- 2 cans light coconut milk
- 2 cups cooked turkey breast, diced
- 2 cups no-sodium chicken broth
- 2 cups butternut squash, peeled, cubed
- 1 cup fresh green beans, diced
- 1 red bell pepper, diced
- 1 medium onion, diced
- 2 tablespoons red curry paste
- 1 tablespoon fresh ginger, grated
- Garnish: lime wedges, pea shoots

Directions

1. Add everything, except lime wedges, and pea shoots, to slow cooker
2. Cover with lid, and cook on LOW 2 hours, until vegetables are tender
3. Serve in bowls, garnish with lime wedges, pea shoots

Nutrition Values (Per Serving)

- Calories: 330
- Fat: 15g
- Carbohydrates: 19g
- Protein: 26g

ROASTED VEGETABLE BROTH

(Prep time: 10 minutes\ Cook time: 6 hours\ 5 Servings)

Ingredients:

- 3 carrots, diced
- 3 parsnips, peeled, diced
- 3 large onions, quartered
- 3 rutabaga, quartered
- 3 bell peppers, halved
- 2 shallots, diced
- 1 whole garlic, diced
- 1 bunch fresh thyme
- 1 bunch fresh parsley
- 5 quarts water

Directions

Preheat oven to 425F

1. Line large baking tray with parchment paper, arrange vegetables in a single layer
2. Drizzle olive oil over vegetables, season with salt and pepper
3. Roast 30 minutes
4. Transfer vegetables to slow cooker
5. Add rest of ingredients, and water
6. Cover with lid, and cook on LOW 6 hours
7. Strain the broth, discard solids

Nutrition Values (Per Serving)

- Calories: 100
- Fat: 0g
- Carbohydrates: 24g
- Protein: 3g

Orzo And Spinach Greek Soup

(Prep time: 10 minutes\ Cook time: 3 hours\ 5 Servings)

Ingredients:

- 2 garlic cloves, minced
- 3 tablespoons lemon juice
- 1 teaspoon lemon zest
- 5 cups chicken broth
- 1 thinly sliced small onion
- 1 cup cooked chicken breast, cubed
- ⅓ cup dried orzo
- 4 cups fresh baby spinach

Directions

1. Add garlic, lemon juice, lemon zest, chicken broth, onion to slow cooker
2. Cover with lid, and cook on LOW 2 hours
3. Stir in cooked chicken, and cook on LOW 30 minutes
4. Add orzo and spinach, stir
5. Simmer 15 minutes
6. Serve in bowls, garnish with fresh dill

Nutrition Values (Per Serving)

- Calories: 150
- Fat: 3g
- Carbohydrates: 16g
- Protein: 14g

CHAPTER 11: APPETIZERS RECIPES

CASHEW MIX

(Prep time: 10 minutes\ Cook time: 2 hours, 30 minutes\ 6 Servings)

Ingredients

- 6 cups cashews
- 3 tablespoons coconut oil
- 1 tablespoon date paste
- Pinch of salt
- 2 tablespoons dried thyme
- 3 tablespoon dried rosemary leaves
- ¾ teaspoon paprika
- ½ teaspoon onion powder
- ½ teaspoon garlic powder

Directions

1. Heat up slow cooker on HIGH for 15 minutes
2. Add cashews, and drizzle coconut oil over top
3. In a small bowl, combine the spices, transfer to slow cooker, toss to evenly coat cashews
4. Cover with lid, and cook on LOW 2 hours, stir every 30 minutes
5. Uncover, and cook 30 more minutes
6. Serve at room temperature

Nutrition Values (Per Serving)

- Calories: 352
- Fat: 21g
- Carbohydrates: 25g
- Protein: 14g

PEPPER AND ALMOND MIX

(Prep time: 10 minutes\ Cook time: 2 hours\ 24 Servings)

Ingredients

- 6 cups whole almonds
- 4 tablespoons ghee
- ½ a teaspoon turmeric
- 1 teaspoon garlic powder
- 1 teaspoon ground black or red peppercorns
- 1 teaspoon ground green peppercorns

Directions

1. Heat up the slow cooker on HIGH setting for 15 minutes
2. Add almonds to slow cooker, drizzle ghee over almonds. Stir to coat evenly
3. Sprinkle garlic powder, turmeric, and peppercorns over the almonds. Stir to coat evenly
4. Cover with lid, and cook on LOW 90 minutes, stirring every 30 minutes
5. After 2 hours, remove lid, increase to HIGH, cook 30 more minutes

Nutrition Values (Per Serving)

- Calories: 127
- Fat: 12g
- Carbohydrates: 14g
- Protein:4g

MUSHROOM MEDLEY

(Prep time: 20 minutes\ Cook time: 2 hours\ 4 Servings)

Ingredients

- 3 cups cremini mushrooms
- 4 garlic cloves, minced
- ½ teaspoon dried basil
- ½ teaspoon dried oregano
- ¼ teaspoon dried thyme
- 1 bay leave
- 1 cup vegetable broth
- ¼ cup coconut milk
- Pinch of sea salt, ground black pepper
- Garnish: fresh parsley

Directions

1. Add mushrooms, garlic, and herbs to slow cooker
2. Pour in vegetable broth, season with salt and pepper
3. Cover with lid, and cook on LOW 2 hours
4. When done, remove lid, stir in coconut milk. Heat to high until sauce thickens
5. Remove bay leaf, serve in a bowl, garnish with fresh parsley

Nutrition Values (Per Serving)

- Calories: 190
- Fat: 1g
- Carbohydrates: 40g
- Protein: 8g

LEMON ARTICHOKES

(Prep time: 10 minutes\ Cook time: 3 hours\ 4 Servings)

Ingredients

- 5 large artichokes
- 1 teaspoon fine sea salt
- 2 celery stalks, minced
- 2 large carrots, sliced into matchsticks
- Juice from ½ a fresh lemon
- ¼ teaspoon black pepper
- 1 teaspoon dried thyme
- 1 tablespoon dried rosemary
- 2 cups boiling water
- Garnish: lemon wedges

Directions

1. Remove the stalk from the artichokes, remove any tough outer shell
2. Transfer artichokes to slow cooker, and pour 2 cups of boiling water
3. Add celery, salt, lemon juice, carrots, thyme, black pepper, and rosemary
4. Cover with lid, and cook on HIGH 3 hours, or until fork tender
5. Serve on a platter, garnish with lemon wedges

Nutrition Values (Per Serving)

- Calories: 190
- Calories: 205
- Fat: 2g
- Carbohydrates: 12g
- Protein: 34g

Dijon Brussel Sprouts

(Prep time: 15 minutes\ Cook time: 3 hours \For 4 Servings)

Ingredients

- 1 pound Brussel sprouts, ends trimmed off
- 1 tablespoon olive oil
- 1½ tablespoon Dijon mustard
- ¼ cup water
- Pinch of salt, pepper
- ½ teaspoon dried tarragon (optional)

Directions

1. Add Brussel sprouts, water, mustard, salt, pepper to slow cooker(and tarragon, if using)
2. Stir well
3. Cover with lid, and cook LOW 3 hours, until fork tender
4. Some Brussels might get crispy
5. Pour in Dijon mustard, stir well
6. Pour in serving bowl, garnish with fresh parsley

Nutrition Values (Per Serving)

- Calories: 83
- Fat: 4g
- Carbohydrates: 11g
- Protein: 4g

SPICY POTATO CHILI

(Prep time: 15 minutes\ Cook time: 4 hours\ 6 Servings)

Ingredients

- 6 large sweet potatoes, peeled, diced
- 2 garlic cloves, minced
- 1 large onion, diced
- 3 cans (28 oz, each) tomato sauce
- 2 can (28 oz) minced tomatoes
- 4 cups vegetable broth
- 1 small can mixed beans, your choice
- 4 tablespoons chili powder
- 2 teaspoons black pepper
- 1 teaspoon oregano
- Garnish: fresh cilantro, tortilla strips, cream

Directions

1. Transfer listed ingredients to slow cooker
2. Stir well
3. Cover with lid, and cook on LOW 4 hours
4. Serve in bowls, garnish with fresh cilantro, tortilla strips, cream

Nutrition Values (Per Serving)

- Calories: 210
- Fat: 8g
- Carbohydrates: 20g
- Protein: 15g

VEGETABLE RATATOUILLE

(Prep time: 20 minutes\ Cook time: 3 hours\ 8 Servings)

Ingredients

- 2 tablespoons coconut oil
- 1 large red onion, chopped
- 6 garlic cloves, minced
- 1 large eggplant, peeled, diced
- 1 large orange bell pepper, diced
- 2 summer squash, peeled, deseeded, diced
- 1 zucchini, peeled, diced
- 1 cup grape tomatoes, halved
- 1 teaspoon dried oregano
- 1 teaspoon ground pepper
- ½ teaspoon sea salt
- ¼ teaspoon crushed red pepper flakes
- 1 can (28 oz) plum tomatoes
- 1 tablespoon balsamic vinegar
- Garnish: fresh basil, chopped

Directions

1. In a large skillet, heat the coconut oil
2. Sauté red onion, garlic, eggplant, bell pepper, squash, zucchini until slightly golden
3. Transfer to slow cooker
4. Stir in plum and halved tomatoes, balsamic vinegar, oregano, pepper, red pepper flakes
5. Cover with lid, and cook on LOW 3 hours, until vegetables fork tender
6. Serve in bowls, garnish with fresh basil

Nutrition Values (Per Serving)

- Calories: 200
- Fat: 3g
- Carbohydrates: 38g
- Protein: 6g

GREEN BEAN CASSEROLE

(Prep time: 15 minutes\ Cook time: 3 hours\ 6 Servings)

Ingredients

- 1 pound green beans, wash, trim ends, dice in even chunks
- 1 cup fresh mushrooms, wipe with damp cloth, slice
- 1 can fat-free cream of mushroom soup
- 1 teaspoon coconut aminos
- ⅛ teaspoon ground black pepper
- 1 cup French's fried onions (crunchy ones)

Directions

1. Grease slow cooker with olive oil
2. Place ingredients in slow cooker, stir
3. Cover with lid, and cook on LOW 3 hours
4. Serve on a platter, garnish with more crunchy fried onions

Nutrition Values (Per Serving)

- Calories: 110
- Fat: 6g
- Carbohydrates: 12g
- Protein: 3g

CRANBERRY BEETS

(Prep time: 5 minutes\ Cook time: 1 hour\ 4 Servings)

Ingredients

- 1 pound cooked beets, quartered
- ⅛ teaspoon of ground nutmeg
- 1 tablespoon date paste
- 2 teaspoons Arrowroot powder
- ½ cup cranberry juice
- 2 teaspoons olive oil
- ½ teaspoon finely shredded orange zest

Directions

1. Add beets to slow cooker and sprinkle nutmeg
2. In a small bowl, combine date paste, arrowroot. Mix well
3. Whisk in cranberry juice
4. Pour over the beets, stir well to evenly coat
5. Cover with lid, and cook on HIGH 1 hour
6. Serve on a platter

Nutrition Values (Per Serving)

- Calories: 110
- Fat: 6g
- Carbohydrates: 12g
- Protein: 3g

Chapter 12: Vegan And Vegetarian Recipes

Vegetable Thai Curry

(Prep time: 15 minutes\ Cook time: 2 hours, 30 minutes\ 6 Servings)

Ingredients

- ½ cauliflower, cut into florets
- 2 medium sweet potatoes, peeled, cubed
- 1 small onion, diced
- 1 can light coconut milk
- 3 tablespoons coconut aminos
- 2 teaspoons siracha sauce
- 3 tablespoons red curry paste
- 1 tablespoon date paste
- 1 cup white mushrooms, quartered
- 1 cup green peas
- Pinch of salt, pepper
- Garnish: toasted cashews, fresh basil leaves, fresh cilantro

Directions

1. Add cauliflower, sweet potatoes, onions to slow cooker
2. In a small bowl, combine coconut milk, coconut aminos, red curry paste, date paste, siracha sauce. Whisk until combined
3. Pour mixture over ingredients in slow cooker
4. Season with salt, pepper
5. Cover with lid, and cook on LOW 2 hours
6. Add mushrooms and peas, cook 30 more minutes
7. Serve over rice, garnish with toasted cashews, basil, and cilantro

Nutrition Values (Per Serving)

- Calories: 518
- Fat: 31g
- Carbohydrates: 57g
- Protein: 13g

CAULIFLOWER BOLOGNESE WITH ZUCCHINI ZOODLES
(Prep time: 10 minutes\ Cook time: 3 hours\ 4 Servings)

Ingredients

- 1 head cauliflower, cut in florets
- 1 small red onion, diced
- 2 garlic cloves, minced
- 1 teaspoon dried basil
- 2 teaspoons oregano flakes
- 2 large cans (2 x 28 oz) diced tomatoes
- ½ cup vegetable broth
- ¼ teaspoon red pepper flakes
- Pinch of salt, pepper
- 5 large zucchini
- Garnish: fresh parsley, parmesan cheese

Directions

1. Add listed ingredients to slow cooker, except zucchini
2. Stir well
3. Cover with lid, and cook on HIGH 3 hours
4. As it cooks, pass zucchini through a spiralizer to make accompanying dish, zoodles
5. Once done, mash a couple times with masher to desired consistency
6. Plate zoodles, cover with cauliflower Bolognese, garnish with parsley, parmesan cheese

Nutrition Values (Per Serving)

- Calories: 316
- Fat: 25g
- Carbohydrates: 7g
- Protein: 13g

SWEET AND SOUR RED CABBAGE

(Prep time: 10 minutes\ Cook time: 4 hours\ 4 Servings)

Ingredients

- ½ a head red cabbage, shredded
- 1 medium red onion, shredded
- 1½ tablespoon date paste
- 1 teaspoon ghee
- ¼ cup water
- ½ cup apple cider vinegar
- 1 tablespoon white wine vinegar
- ½ teaspoon fresh ground black pepper
- ¼ teaspoon salt
- ⅛ teaspoon ground cloves
- ½ teaspoon thyme

Directions

1. Add listed ingredients to slow cooker
2. Stir well
3. Cover with lid, and cook on LOW 4 hours, until cabbage is tender
4. Serve on a platter

Nutrition Values (Per Serving)

- Calories: 60
- Fat: 1g
- Carbohydrates: 13g
- Protein: 2g

GINGER SWEET POTATOES

(Prep time: 10 minutes\ Cook time: 2 hours\ 10 Servings)

Ingredients

- 2½ pounds sweet potatoes, peeled, diced
- 1 cup of water
- 1-inch fresh ginger, peeled, grated
- ½ tablespoon ghee
- Salt and pepper
- Garnish: fresh parsley

Directions

1. Place potatoes in slow cooker
2. Add water, fresh ginger. Stir well
3. Cover with lid, and cook on HIGH 2 hours, until potatoes are tender
4. Once cooked, drain any water
5. Add ghee, and mash the potatoes
6. Season with salt and pepper
7. Serve in a bowl, garnish with fresh parsley

Nutrition Values (Per Serving)

- Calories: 100
- Fat: 0.5g
- Carbohydrates: 23g
- Protein: 2g

STEWED TOMATOES

(Prep time: 10 minutes\ Cook time: 3 hours\ 6 Servings)

Ingredients

- 2 cans (28 oz) whole tomatoes
- 1 small onion, minced
- 1 garlic clove, minced
- 2 celery stalks, diced
- 1 teaspoon oregano
- 1 teaspoon of thyme
- Garnish: fresh cilantro

Directions

1. Add listed ingredients to slow cooker. Stir well
2. Cover with lid, and cook on LOW 3 hours
3. Serve on a platter, garnish with cilantro

Nutrition Values (Per Serving)

- Calories: 100
- Fat: 0.5g
- Carbohydrates: 23g
- Protein: 2g

DILL CARROTS

(Prep time: 10 minutes\ Cook time: 2 hours\ 6 Servings)

Ingredients

- 1 pound carrots, sliced
- 1 tablespoon fresh dill, minced
- ½ teaspoon ghee
- 3 tablespoons water

Directions

1. Add ingredients to slow cooker
2. Stir well
3. Cover with lid, and cook on LOW 2 hours, until carrots are tender
4. Serve on a platter, garnish with fresh parsley

Nutrition Values (Per Serving)

- Calories: 35
- Fat: 0g
- Carbohydrates: 8g
- Protein: 1g

GARLIC MASHED POTATOES

(Prep time: 5 minutes\ Cook time: 2 hours\ 10 Servings)

Ingredients

- 3 pounds red skin potatoes, peeled, cubed
- 4 garlic cloves, minced
- 1 cup chicken broth
- ¼ cup almond milk
- 1 tablespoon ghee
- ⅓ cup cashew cream
- Salt and pepper to season
- Garnish: fresh parsley

Directions

1. Add potatoes, garlic, chicken broth to slow cooker
2. Stir well
3. Cover with lid, and cook on LOW 2 hours, until potatoes are fork tender
4. Once cooked, drain off any liquid
5. Mash the potatoes, add the almond milk, cashew cream. Stir
6. Season with salt and pepper
7. Serve in a bowl, garnish with fresh parsley

Nutrition Values (Per Serving)

- Calories: 130
- Fat: 2g
- Carbohydrates: 23g
- Protein: 4g

STEWED SQUASH

(Prep time: 10 minutes\ Cook time: 3 hours\ 4 Servings)

Ingredients

- 1 medium yellow onion, ¼ inch slices
- 3 cups zucchini, peeled, sliced
- 1 tablespoon fresh dill
- 3 tablespoons lemon juice
- 1 teaspoon of ghee
- Salt and pepper to season
- Garnish: fresh dill

Directions

1. Place sliced onion along bottom of slow cooker
2. Cover with zucchini, dill lemon juice, salt, pepper
3. Cover with lid, and cook on LOW 3 hours
4. Open slow cooker, add ghee. Stir
5. Recover with lid, and cook on HIGH 30 minutes

Nutrition Values (Per Serving)

- Calories: 70
- Fat: 2g
- Carbohydrates: 14g
- Protein: 2g

STEWED OKRA

(Prep time: 10 minutes\ Cook time: 3 hours\ 4 Servings)

Ingredients

- 2 large tomatoes, diced
- 1½ cups okra, diced
- 1 small onion, diced
- 2 garlic cloves, minced
- 1 teaspoon hot sauce

Directions

1. Add listed ingredients to slow cooker
2. Stir well
3. Cover with lid, and cook on LOW 3 hours
4. Serve on a platter

Nutrition Values (Per Serving)

- Calories: 40
- Fat: 0g
- Carbohydrates: 8g
- Protein: 2g

CHAPTER 13: A LITTLE EXTRA RECIPES

While these recipes do not require a slow cooker, they can be a great accompaniment to any recipe.

WHOLE30 BREADCRUMBS

(Prep time: 5 minutes\ Cook time: 0 minutes\ 4 Servings)

Ingredients

- 1 cup almond flour/meal
- ½ teaspoon sea salt
- ½ teaspoon black pepper
- ½ teaspoon garlic powder
- ½ teaspoon dried parsley
- ¼ teaspoon onion powder
- ¼ teaspoon dried oregano

Directions

1. In a medium bowl, combine the ingredients. Whisk to combine
2. Use as needed

Nutrition Values (Per Serving)

- Calories: 528
- Fat: 2g
- Dietary Fiber: 1g
- Protein: 57g

Whole30 Sour Cream

(Prep time: 5 minutes\ Cook time: 0 minutes\ 4 Servings)

Ingredients

- 1 can unsweetened coconut milk
- 1½ tablespoons lemon juice
- ½ tablespoon apple cider vinegar
- ⅛ teaspoon salt

Directions

1. Place can of coconut milk in fridge overnight
2. Flip can upside down, open, pour off liquid
3. Scrape out the thick cream, place in a bowl
4. Combine with lemon juice, salt, vinegar
5. Whisk until smooth
6. Use when needed

Nutrition Values (Per Serving)

- Calories: 129
- Fat: 15g
- Dietary Fiber: 1g
- Protein: 4g

WHOLE30 MAYONNAISE

(Prep time: 5 minutes\ Cook time: 0 minutes\ 4 Servings)

Ingredients

- 1 egg
- ½ teaspoon sea salt
- ½ teaspoon ground mustard
- 1¼ cup extra light olive oil
- 1 tablespoon lemon juice

Directions

1. Place egg, ground mustard, salt, ¼ cup of olive oil in food processor
2. Mix on low until combined
3. As processor turns, drizzle in remaining olive oil. Mix 3 minutes, until thickens
4. Drizzle in lemon juice, pulse on low until fully combined
5. Chill 30 minutes before using

Nutrition Values (Per Serving)

- Calories: 176
- Fat: 16g
- Dietary Fiber: 1g
- Protein: 6g

WHOLE30 KETCHUP

(Prep time: 5 minutes\ Cook time: 0 minutes\ 4 Servings)

Ingredients

- ½ cup chopped pitted dates
- 1 can (6 oz) tomato paste
- 1 can (14 oz) diced tomatoes
- 2 tablespoons coconut vinegar
- ½ cup bone broth
- 1 teaspoon garlic powder
- 1 teaspoon onion powder
- 1 teaspoon salt
- ½ teaspoon cayenne pepper

Directions

1. Add ingredients to small saucepan
2. Cook on medium-low 20 minutes
3. Turn off heat
4. Using an immersion blender, pulse until smooth
5. Simmer on low 10 minutes
6. Cool completely before using

Nutrition Values (Per Serving)

- Calories: 263
- Fat: 1g
- Dietary Fiber: 2g
- Protein: 2g

WHOLE30 WORCESTERSHIRE SAUCE

(Prep time: 5 minutes\ Cook time: 15 minutes\ 4 Servings)

Ingredients

- ½ cup apple cider vinegar
- 2 tablespoons water
- 2 tablespoons coconut aminos
- ¼ teaspoon mustard seeds
- ¼ teaspoon onion powder
- ¼ teaspoon garlic powder
- ⅛ teaspoon cinnamon
- ⅛ teaspoon black pepper

Directions

1. Add listed ingredients to medium saucepan
2. Bring to a boil, and stir well
3. Simmer 5 minutes
4. Cool completely before using

Nutrition Values (Per Serving)

- Calories: 170
- Fat: 1g
- Dietary Fiber: 1g
- Protein: 6g

WHOLE30 BBQ SAUCE

(Prep time: 5 minutes\ Cook time: 5 minutes\ 4 Servings)

Ingredients

- ¼ cup balsamic vinegar
- ½ cup water
- 1 can (8 oz) tomato paste
- 8 pitted Medjool dates
- 2 tablespoons Dijon mustard
- 2 tablespoons coconut aminos
- ½ teaspoon garlic powder
- ½ teaspoon onion powder
- ½ teaspoon salt
- ½ teaspoon pepper

Directions

1. Add listed ingredients to a medium saucepan
2. Simmer over low heat 5 minutes
3. Transfer sauce to blender, process on high 2 minutes
4. May need to add a bit of water for desired consistency
5. Cool completely before using

Nutrition Values (Per Serving)

- Calories: 170
- Fat: 2g
- Dietary Fiber: 1g
- Protein: 3g

WHOLE30 TACO SEASONING

(Prep time: 5 minutes\ Cook time: 0 minutes\ 4 Servings)

Ingredients

- 1 tablespoon chili powder
- ½ a teaspoon garlic powder
- ½ a teaspoon onion powder
- 1½ teaspoon ground cumin
- 1 teaspoon salt
- 1 teaspoon pepper
- ¼ teaspoon red pepper flakes
- ¼ teaspoon dried oregano
- ½ teaspoon paprika

Directions

1. Combine listed ingredients in a glass jar
2. Shake until combined (jar can be used for storing)
3. Use as needed

Nutrition Values (Per Serving)

- Calories: 100
- Fat: 0g
- Dietary Fiber: 2g
- Protein: 0g

WHOLE30 FAJITA SEASONING

(Prep time: 5 minutes\ Cook time: 0 minutes\ 4 Servings)

Ingredients

- ¼ cup chili powder
- 2 tablespoons ground cumin
- 1 tablespoon salt
- 4 teaspoons black pepper
- 3 teaspoons dried oregano
- 2 teaspoons paprika
- 1 teaspoon onion powder
- 1 teaspoon parsley

Directions

1. Combine ingredients in a glass jar
2. Shake until combined (jar can be used for storing)
3. Use as needed

Nutrition Values (Per Serving)

- Calories: 100
- Fat: 0g
- Dietary Fiber: 0g
- Protein: 0g

CONCLUSION

I would like to thank you again for purchasing the book and taking the time of going through it ! I do hope this book has been helpful and you found the information contained within useful.

Keep in mind that you are not only limited to the recipes provided in this book. Keep exploring until you find the best Whole30 regime that works for you.

Stay healthy and stay safe!

Printed in the USA
CPSIA information can be obtained
at www.ICGtesting.com
LVHW011823091123
763047LV00111B/167